"Om Aim Sa

May Mother Saraswatee bless you with Divine knowledge
and inspire you to taste the nectar of Divine Bliss through the
chanting and singing of God's names and glories

Bhajans, Kirtans, Shlokas & Chants
First Published in 1989
Revised Edition Published 1991
by
Nada Productions Inc.

This Revised and Enlarged Edition
is published by
Nada Productions Inc.
2216 NW 8th Terrace, Fort Lauderdale FL, 33311
1999

Ph 1-800-964-2553 outside US 954-563-4946
Web Site www.yogihari.com
E-Mail: yogihari@aol.com

The Bhajans, Kirtans, Shlokas
&
Chants

Yogi Hari

Nada Productions Inc
2216 NW 8th Terrace, Fort Lauderdale, Florida 33311 U.S.A

Nada Productions Inc.
2216 NW 8th Terrace, Fort Lauderdale FL, 33311

Cover and layout design by Robert Moses
Printed in The United States of America
Published by Nada Productions Inc.

Library of Congress Cataloging-in-Publication Data
Bhajans, Kirtans, Shlokas & Chants ISBN: 1-57777-050-1

Cover and layout design by Robert Moses
Printed in The United States of America
and Published by Nada Productions Inc.

I am eternally grateful to my music master Swami Nadabrahmanandaji for his divine gift of music and to my Guru, Swami Vishnu Devanandaji for his constant inspiration and guidance on my spiritual path. To my wife, Leela Mata for her unswerving support and encouragement.

ACKNOWLEDGEMENTS

In this third edition, I wish to thank Br. Darshanand and Dr. Doshi for their dilligent assistance in refining the transliteration and meaning.

Swami Shankarananda (Robert Moses) for design and layout. Each one of them worked selflessly and with much love.

CONTENTS

BHAJANS 1

BHAJANS 2

NADA MALA FOR MASTER SHIVANANDA

ADORATIONS TO RAMA

ADORATIONS TO DIVINE MOTHER

ADORATIONS TO SHIVA AND SHIVA BHAJANS

SHIVA CHANTS

ADORATIONS TO KRISHNA

KRISHNA BHAJANS

ADORATIONS TO LORD NARAAYANA

WINGS OF LIBERATION

OH MAN OH MIND

ANANADA

.I have had the rare opportunity to know Yogi Hari almost all my life, for he is my husband. It is a difficult challenge to write of someone you know so closely, yet all it requires is simple honesty.

Bhajans, Kirtans, Shlokas and Chants is a product of Yogi Hari's consummate yearning for music since childhood. The sound of his mother's voice singing and humming while he was a baby created deep impressions in his mind and must have awakened past Samskaras, for he was fascinated by the intriguing world of sound ever since. As a little boy, the chants at the village temple charmed his mind. It was there that his love of chanting God's name through bhajan, kirtan and shlokas began. As a teenager, the songs of Lata Mangeshkar, Mukesh, Manaday, Mohamed Rafi, and other film artists captured his imagination. This led him to singing on the national radio station where he was one of the youngest talents. At that time Yogi Hari had had no formal training in music. He had learned by ear; first listening and later imitating what was heard. His blossoming talent as a singer, though unschooled, was due to his meticulous attention to timing. Back then he used to keep time by clicking his teeth. They were the drum right in his head.

Yogi Hari's first instrument was an accordion he acquired when he was 21 years old. Unfortunately he didn't know how to play it and there was no teacher. Attempting to make music on the accordion caused his increasingly gnawing desire to find a teacher and study music in a systematic manner. This desire was fulfilled in 1975 when he met his music master, Swami Nadabrahmananda in the Bahamas. By supreme grace, God and Guru, music became his sadhana and a constant focus of attention.

Yogi Hari's dedication to music can best be described as an insatiable hunger. Meeting Swami Nadabrahmananda was God's answer to his fervent and voiceless prayers. We were already the parents of four children, but having a family did not stop us from living a nomadic lifestyle traveling from place to place so that Yogi Hari could be near his master and learn from him. This was a period of heroic growth and challenge. He was playing the many different roles of father, husband, student, and disciple all at once, and all in a foreign land. It was tremendously challenging for all of us, especially the children, who had to adapt and adjust every time they went to a different school by making new friends and starting over again. Later we were to understand that this was not just about learning music, but about the transformation of an ordinary individual into an extraordinary human being.

Listening to Yogi Hari's music is a marvelous experience and it is also a helpful tool for meditation. Every morning I listen to his practice and I can truly say that it has given me the power to transcend my body and mind and enter into blissful states for over two hours at a time. Meditation becomes very easy when listening to these divine songs. Bhajans, Kirtans, Shlokas and Chants is not just a book, but it is the fruit of tremendous sadhana and loving dedication to God, Guru, and humanity.

It has been a blessing for me to be a part of this and may it be a blessing to you as well.

LEELA MATA

This garland of music that I offer to God in my Sadhana, I now make available to you. As one gathers flowers with love and devotion for Puja (worship), so have I collected these Bhajans, Kirtans, Shlokas and Chants, from my music master Swami Nadabrahmanandaji Maharaj and many other sources; from our ancient scriptures like the Vedas, Upanishads, Ramayana, etc. and the great Gyani and Bhakta Saints like Adi Shankaracharya, Tukaram, Kabir, Tulsidas, Mirabai etc., and sang them in Ragas and Talas that inspire devotion for God They lift the mind out of depression, anxiety and restlessness and transport it to Divine ecstacy.

As I am immersed in God Intoxication through the singing and chanting of God's name, so will you, to a great measure, be inspired as you listen and sing .

This is made possible by the various recordings on CD's and audio tapes and this book with the transliteration and meaning. If you play the harmonium or tabla and understand fundamentals of Hindustani Classical Music - Ragas and Talas - you will greatly benefit from this project.

It is with great love and persistence that I have been able to complete this valuable gift to my fellow aspirants and will continue to add to this as I grow in His service through Nada Yoga. May it serve to gladden your heart and inspire devotion and love for God.

Yogi Hari
June, 1999

Nada Yoga is the science of using vibration to connect with God, or Brahman, the one without a second, or the all pervading consciousness. Brahman manifests in this universe as vibration. This first manifestation of the absolute is referred to as Om or Nada Brahman. It is the immutable essence underlying all creation. This is the highest state of divine vibration and is referred to as the Para state. This vibration then becomes differentiated into the primordial elements of sattwa, rajas and tamas. These are the gunas, which form the building blocks of all creation. The gunas compose the Pashyanti state, or second level of divine vibration. These first two vibrational states of Para and Pashyanti are of the realm of transcendence and can only be experienced through deep meditation. The third level of differentiated vibration exists in the mental plane in the form of thought; something that can be concieved in the mind. It is referred to as Madyama. The fourth state of vibration is manifest in the external physical world as audible sound, and is referred to as Vaikhari. The music we hear played on instruments or vocal music for example, is of the fourth state and is only the gross manifestation of vibration. Nada Yoga uses divine music to move from gross diferentiated vibrations to sublte vibrations and eventually into the para state, where God is experienced directly as Nadam.

The music created by saints and yogis has a positive effect on the mind. As one participates in the music by singing with devotion, divine impressions are created in the mind. As the mind is made calm and peaceful by the renderings of such lofty souls, it is able to transcend the Vaikari and Madyama states of vibration, going beyond audible sounds and mental conceptions. This is when one may enter the second vibrational state of Pashyanti, where the anahata sound is heard. Anahata is the state of divine intuition which is caused by the vibration of akash, or ether. The mind does not even posses the ability to conceive the glory of the Anahata sound until it is experienced through transcendence. Eventually the devotee who is absorbed in the anahata sound will be lead to the Para State. Para is the highest of vibrations, it is the source of direct experience of God.

Patanjali says of God: "In him knowledge is infinite, in others it is only a germ. He was the teacher of even the earliest teachers, since he is not limited by time. The word which expresses him is Om. This word must be repeated with meditation on its meaning. Hence comes knowledge of the purusha and destruction of the obstacles to knowledge." In Katha Upanishad it is written: "This syllable Om is Brahman. This syllable is indeed supreme. It is the strongest support. It is the highest symbol. He who knows it is reverenced as a knower of Brahman." In our practice, Om precedes all the names or mantras of God. The names of God are many, but in each and every name, be it Rama, Christ, Krishna, Allah, or Buddha, the power of God abides.

The sadhana of chanting the name of God is very simple, with no stringent rules set to reap it's benefits. It can be done at any time, in any place, and in any situation. No specific rites are required. The name of God can be repeated silently, quietly, or loudly. Each method is beneficial. But chanting in a resounding voice, purifies not only the individual but his whole environment. The divine name can be chanted alone or in groups. When chanting alone the energy generated may be compared to a ripple on the water, but in a consolidated group the energy created is like that of a huge tidal wave bearing the power to drown out all negativity and mental agitation, leaving divine Bhava in its wake. The Lord said: "I dwell not in Vaikunta nor in the hearts of yogins, but I dwell where my devotees sing my name, Oh Narada." From this assurance one should diligently take up the singing and hearing of the glory of God. Even while engaged in the ordinary activities of life, this will bring the taste of divine bliss. It can become the habit of the learned and the ignorant alike, and should the ignorant develop the habit of chanting the Lord's name, they will no longer remain in ignorance, but will become the embodiment of knowledge.

The name of God is mantra. It is divine energy encased in a structure of sound. It is the formula of a specific manifestation of God. A mantra has five specific qualities: (1) a definite meter or rhythm, (2) a specific shakti or energy, (3) a presiding deity or manifestation of God, (4) a Rishi to whom this mantra was revealed (who used it to realize God and in turn handed it down to humanity through his disciples), and (5) a mantra also has a kalika or pin that locks the energy (this is why each person has to do the Sadhana necessary to unlock the energy in order to have the siddhi of the mantra and also to have the darshan of the Ishta Devata that the mantra represents).

The language of mantra is Sanskrit, or devanagari: language of the Gods. It is the most ancient and mystic of human languages. It is the source from which all other laguages evolved. Mantras can be translated from the Sanskrit, but their translations do not have the same power because Sanskrit came as vibration from the source of creation. The Mantras are made up of root sounds, which are the actual vibrations arising from the object or action for which they are used. For example, the root sound "ma" means mother. This sound is a Mantra representing the God aspect of the mother. It is the sound with which a child instictively calls for its mother.

In the subtle body, each of the seven chakras (energy centers within the body) has a particular number of petals with a Sanskrit root sound manifesting the energy of each petal. Thus in singing Sanskrit mantras glorifying God, the chakras are stimulated and the subtle energy is awakened. This is one reason mantra chanting is the easiest of all modes of approaching God: it purifies and harmonizes the energy systems in the body, making it a fit vehicle for the transcendent vision of God. The various musical notes also have their own corresponding subtle channels in the Chakras. Music vibrates these channels, purifies them and awakens the psychic and spiritual power dormant in them.

Name and form are like the two sides of a coin; you cannot have one without the other. When you repeat a name, the form comes to mind. Although you may not consciously know the form connected with a certain Mantra, it still creates a specific thought pattern in the mind. The thought patterns created by Mantras are positive, beneficial, and calming. In this the Kali Yuga (Iron Age), chanting God's name is the best Yoga. There is power in every word. Even as the name of an object in this world generates the consciousness of the object in the mind, the name of God generates God-consciousness and purifies mind. The name becomes the direct cause of the realization of the highest perfection of God. He who constantly chants the name of God forgets the world and merges into super-consciousness.

BHAJAN

Bhajans are poems set to music and sung with love and devotion. Bhajans glorify God in all aspects, qualities, and manifestations so that love and devotion is invoked for him. The poetry of bhajan is either devotional or philosophical in nature. It reminds us that this life is the most valuable treasure one can posses and that every moment should be utilized to reach the true goal and purpose of life, which is God Realization or Self

Realization. A bhajan reminds you of your real nature. It reminds you that you are not the body and mind, but that you are the spirit, the soul, the immortal self, or atman. It gives us an understanding of how to relate and to live in this world so that we may constantly evolve and grow. It says that this body and mind are instruments and gifts from God. They are to be used in the service of God and humanity for the sole purpose of reaching moksha or liberation.

Self Realized Saints and Nada Yogis express their love for God and humanity in the form of poetry. These masters condense and summarize the complex and intricate philosophies of Vedanta in a few verses. This kind of poetry is found in all major religions and cultures that reach for the profound understanding of "Self." These poems are set to music in appropriate ragas (melodies), and talas (rhythmic patterns), to invoke love and devotion for God. When rendered by a nada yogi, saint, or spiritual aspirant, bhajan has the ability to heal the body and to lift the mind out of depression. It relieves restless anxiety and leaves one in a state of joyfulness and peace. On bhajan, Master Sivananda has written: "Bhajan is meditation on God. Bhajan is upasana (worship). In short, all contrivances or methods that are calculated to bring the devotee face to face with God are Bhajan. Japa (repetition of His name), Sankirtan (singing His name alone or with a party), and prayer constitute Bhajan. Life without Bhajan of some sort or another is useless my dear friend. Life without worship is dreary and cheerless. It is a mere burden on this earth. Just as zero is nothing without one, so also this life is practically nothing without Bhajan."

KIRTAN - SANKIRTAN

Kirtan is the singing of God's name with the feeling of divine love. Such singing has a benign effect on both the physical and subtle bodies. It is an excellent method of soothing the nerves and directing the emotions toward a positive goal. While the Mantras are in Sanskrit, the Kirtans can be sung in any language. For example, Christian hymns are considered Kirtan. Kirtan becomes Sankirtan when two or more people get together to chant the name of God with love and devotion. Sometimes one person will lead and the others respond. At other times they all sing together. Kirtan is richly embellished by the addition of musical instruments.

In Satsanga, where people gather for meditation, for ritual worship, to seek God's guidance, to listen to philosophical discourses and prayers, and in functions where religious ceremonies are to be performed, Sankirtan should be done first. Sankirtan creates a divine atmosphere that calms and focuses the mind. It has the power to make these occasions much more meaningful. When all the participants sing from the bottom of their hearts, casting aside inhibition and reservation, something magical happens: the level of divine vibration multiplies and rises, taking the mind to the state where it experiences bliss that transcends rational thought, reason, and earthly sensual pleasures. A mysterious transformation takes place on the physical, mental and emotional levels. A strong upward current lifts everyone to heights that are difficult to reach as an individual, especially if one is a beginer on the spiritual path. Those who participate fully, drink of the sweetness of bliss that is produced from this mystic practice. Gatherings like these can be the greatest therapy and healing force, not only for the individauls participating, but on a more subtle level, all of creation becomes positively aligned to its essential vibrational level of Satchidananda (existence, knowledge and bliss absolute.)

The word shloka comes from the verbal root "shlok," meaning to collect. Shloka is the medium via which a Sanskrit poet collects and composes his thoughts. Shlokas can be composed in different meters and every meter has a specific way to chant. The topics of shlokas differ. There are those that sing God's praise and glory, others teach morals and ethics, and some reveal mystic knowledge of the yogis, saints and sages. Shlokas teach us to uplift and elevate our consciousness, beautify our speech, and enrich our lives. They help us to collect our thoughts and focus them on the changeless eternal supreme Lord.

God is immanent and transcendent. The seers in the Isha Upanishads declare that "In dark night live those for whom God is transcendent only, and darker still for whom he is immanent only. But those who know him as immanent and transcendent cross the sea of death with the immanent and enter into immortality with the transcendent." One can only reach the transcendent through the immanent. Even though God is pure consciousness; one without the second; the all pervading reality, these are only abstract concepts and ideas for the mind. For those who function only through the body-mind-intellect equipment which experiences only the waking, dream and deep sleep state, the transcendent has not yet become the reality of existence. In the process of reaching for the higher reality, the mind needs something it can relate to; something more concrete This is where a personal relationship with God is most helpful. Until the transcendental experience of God is reached, God can only be conceived as Ishwara, or Brahman conditioned by maya.

The science of Japa, or mantra repetition, has been prescribed by the great yogis and rishis for those who long for liberation. When chanting and repeating a Mantra vocally or mentally, contact is made with a specific manifestation of God or Ishta Devata (chosen ideal). When one listens to mantra, the mind becomes focused and concentrated on the divine vibration. Eventually you want to chant along and the mantra makes such a deep impression in the mind that it remains there all day long. This will makes one feel happy and it transforms the personality in subtle ways. When chanting a mantra like Om Shri Ram Jaya Ram Jaya Jaya Ram Om, the presence and blessings of Lord Rama are invoked. The mind is also visualizing Rama and associating with all his good qualities. As one becomes familiar with the incarnation of Rama, his life, his teaching, and his mission, devotion for God through the personality of Rama increases. As emotions are being transformed into devotion, there is experience the of a higher state of awareness in which the heart and mind become purified and uplifted. At this time the mind is less agitated. This makes sitting for meditation much easier and eventually the limitations of body and mind are transcended. This is when God is experienced directly. This is the fourth state of consciousness. It lies beyond sleeping, waking and dreaming. It is called Samadhi. In this state you experience that you are the spirit, the soul, the atman, and that you are truly divine. This is what Jesus meant when he said "I and my father are one." This is enlightenment and freedom; the joy of existence.

Kabir once summarized his spiritual practice by saying "All I do is detach and attach." This is simply a matter of constantly detaching the mind from the world and attaching it to God. By chanting and singing the name of God, you are constantly doing this. This is a most practical way to be in the abiding presence of the Lord.

The moksha mantras which Yogi Hari has arranged in ragas and talas, and has made available through various recordings will prove helpful to charm the mind to think of God all the time. May God bless you with peace, joy and divine bliss

LEELA MATA

Leela Mata has been practicing yoga and meditation since childhood. She has been teaching since 1975, and has given many seminars and lectures in the US and abroad. Together with her husband, Yogi Hari, she directs the Sampoorna Yoga Ashram in Ft. Lauderdale.

Her inspiring discourses on life and living can be heard every Sunday at the Center during Satsang. Leela Mata has years of experience and knowledge as a meditator, householder mother of four and grand mother of four. She has recently completed a 2-year program at the Ayurvedic Institute of New Mexico, under the tutelage of Dr. Vasant Lad, the leading authority on Ayurveda in the West.

YOGI HARI

Yogi Hari is an experienced Yoga Master of many talents who has taught extensively in North America, South America, South Africa, Zimbabwe,Europe And Great Britain 1969. Since the age of 20 Yogiji has been searching, experimenting with and practicing Yoga as an art of self-development. He is a living testimony to the value of Yoga as an incomparable science for radiant health and well being. He is a very rare combination of Hatha, Raja, Jnana, Karma Nada and Bhakti Yoga.

In 1975 this searching led him to his Guru Swami Vishnu Devananda and his Music Master Swami Nadabrahmananda. This meeting brought about a new beginning in Yogiji's life, which has ever since blossomed and bore many precious fruits - fruits that are satisfying the hunger of many aspirants all around the world.

Yogi Hari has so far produced 22 audio tapes of Chanting, Bhajans, Kirtan, Mantras and Slokas and has compiled this book with the transliteration and meaning of the music on all of the tapes.

Yogiji's Bhajans and Kirtans bring about peace and joy in the hearts of the listeners. The soul stirring philosophies of the songs, sung in melodious Raga and Tala quietens the mind and lifts it to the highest planes of bliss.

Hatha Yoga is another of the expertise of Yogi Hari, who firmly believes that a healthy and strong body is necessary on the path of self-development. The Hatha Yoga productions are given the same care in orchestration as the musical tapes. The result is an experience of health and peace in body and mind.

Students all over the world who have the "Yoga at Home with Yogi

Hari" video series have found them to be the best Yoga videos on the market.

Regular classes, Yoga Teachers Training Courses, Week long Sadhana Programs and Satsang are given by Yogiraj at his Ashram in Fort Lauderdale, Florida. Yogiji's teachings in all its different aspects lead to the one goal of living the Life Divine right here and now through a healthy body, mind and high aspirations.

WORDS OF BLESSINGS

SATGURU SANT KESHAVADAS

Kirtan or singing in praise of God is the "way" to realize God in this Kali-Yuga - declares Srimad Bhagavatam - the holy scripture of India. "Kalau Tad Harikirtanat". In Kali Yuga God is attained through kirtan. "Kalau Sankirtya Keshavam". Songs in praise of God is the meditation for Kali Yuga - all these are the emphatic declarations in Bhagavatam about the efficacy of Kirtan .

Kirtan is glorification of God. It contains the stories and glories, philosophy and love of God. One important aspect of Kirtan is known as "Bhajan". Bhajan is to take refuge in God and to chant or sing His Holy Name.

Our dear Sri Yogi Hari, is a dedicated devotee of God and Guru. The outcome of his intense Sadhana are his books and beautiful cassettes. In this holy book called, "Bhajans, Kirtan Slokas and Chants", Yogi Hari has clearly written the words, the music, melody and rhythms, the translation in English and he has sung these songs in various cassettes also.

This is the wonderful contribution especially on songs and hymns on God to the Western world. This book has clarity and serves a great pur-

pose for a true Sadhaka or an aspirant to know the truth.

I pray to God to bless Yogi Hari with long life to continue his good work of spreading the Name Divine. I strongly recommend this book for all those devotees who are striving after God-Realization.

SWAMI NADABRAH-MANANDA

Was one of the greatest classical Indian musicians of his time. He was a brilliant vocalist and master of Tabla and Harmoniumand the Swaramandala. He perfected the science of

Taan,Mantra chanting and Bhajans. Swamiji took mahasamadhi at the age of 98. He was a delight to be with: loving, simple and open. A truly holy man, he was a pure channel for the teaching of his art. His very presence created an atmosphere of joy.

Swami Nadabrahmananda was born May 5, 1896 in Mysore State, South India. He began his formal musical training at the age of 20, and continued seventeen years of arduous discipline and austerity under three illustrious masters: Sri Sadashiva Bua of Nargund (Karnataka), Ustad Alladia Khan of Kolhapur and Tata Bua of Benares. During these years he practised as much as twenty hours a day and observed frequent fasts and seclusions to develop intense control and concentration. He became professor of music at the University of Benares and ultimately was appointed court musician for the Maharaja of Mysore State. His fame spread throughout India and he received numerous commercial offers, but in accordance with a vow made to his Guru, he steadfastly refused to compromise the purity of his classical form.

In 1950 in accordance with Indian religious tradition, Swami Nadabrahmananda retired and took the vows of Sanyas. At the ashram of the great sage Sri Swami Sivananda, founder of the Divine Life Society, Rishikesh, Himalayas, he devoted his time to the perfection of music as Nada Yoga, a spiritual practice towards God realization. Then, in 1974, at the behest of many devotees and spiritual organizations, he consented to come to the West, and gave concerts and musical instructions throughout the United States, Canada, the Caribbean and parts of South America. He was a delightful and patient teacher.

Swami Nadabrahmananda also exhibited abilities that were astounding to the western mind. Indian musicians from ancient times have paid much attention to the nature of vibration, its relation to sound, and its effects on the body. This knowledge has been developed into the exact science of Taan, of which Swamiji was the last known master. He exhibited the extraordinary ability to control the rate and location of sound vibrations in his body. He was able to synchronize his voice with complex rapid note changes and direct sound vibrations so that they emanated from points in the mouth, nose, skull and spine. The most difficult of all Taans is the Kundalini Taan, where vibrations issue solely from the base of the spinal column (Muladhaara Chakra); this was achieved by Swamiji after seven years of practice and his initiation by Swami Sivananda into sanyas. His mastery of Taan accounts for his astonishing good health and energy. Another remarkable consequence of his yogic control was his ability to suspend his breathing and not blink his eyes while playing Tabla for half an hour.

Swami Nadabrahmananda's abilities were verified in a number of laboratory experiments both in India and in the West. There were other interesting results from these tests: Dr. Thelma Moss of UCLA, was particularly intrigued by the changes in emanations from Swamiji's fingers before and after performing as made visible by Kirlian photography. At Ottawa University, studies over a three day period showed that Swami Nadabrahmananda did not dream. Elmer Green, PhD., of the Menninger Foundation reported, "While wired to our portable psycho-physiology lab, he demonstrated an important kind of central nervous system control (evidenced by the production and maintenance of alpha and theta brain wave patterns) normally associated with a state of quiet reverie, while he was performing a complex and demanding raga, a musical performance." In another test before a gathering of political and spiritual leaders at the International Yoga Teachers' Congress in the Bahamas, Swamiji demonstrated his con-

trol over bodily functions by consciously raising his blood pressure to 240.
This was when Yogi Hari met Swamiji who accepted him as his disciple and initiated him into the practice of Nada Yoga. Yogi Hari was determined

trol over bodily functions by consciously raising his blood pressure to 240.

This was when Yogi Hari met Swamiji who accepted him as his disciple and initiated him into the practice of Nada Yoga. Yogi Hari was determined to master the science of Nada Yoga, so he followed Swamiji wherever he went in the West and learned from him constantly. Even when Swamiji went back to India, Yogiji would go every year to Rishikesh to continue his studies with his Master.

Swami Nadabrahmananda represented a rare integrity and authenticity of spiritual tradition now virtually lost in the rapid popularization of Indian music. Swamiji's public programs (Satsangs) consisted of demonstrations of Nada Yoga techniques and methods of physical and mental control through music. The songs he presented were classical compositions intended for meditation and devotion.

SWAMI VISHNU DEVANANDA

Swami Vishnudevananda was born in Kerala, in 1927. As a young man he became a lieutenant in the Indian army, but his whole life soon changed when he met Swami Sivananda. At the age of 20, he joined the Divine Life Society in Rishikesh and served as the professor of Hatha Yoga at the Sivananda Yoga Vedanta Forest Academy. There he trained many Indians as well as westerners in the ancient practice of Hatha Yoga. At the request of his Guru, Swami Vishnudevenanda later embarked on a world tour to spread the ideal of Yoga. In 1958 he founded the Sivananda Yoga Vedenta Center in Montreal, and later went on to establish many Yoga centers and ashrams around the world.

In 1975 Swamji convened the Yoga Teachers Congress in the Bahamas, which Yogi Hari attended with his family. Two weeks later while staying at the ashram, Swamiji invited Yogi Hari, then 30 years old and working as a land surveyor, to be part of the Sivananda family. For the next seven years the family lived, studied, and practiced yoga at the various Sirvananda Ashrams in North America.

MASTER SIVANANDA

Born on the 8th of September, 1887, to an illustrious family, Sri Swami Sivananda had a natural flair for a life devoted to the study and practice of Vedanta. Added to this, was an inborn eagerness to serve all, and an innate feeling of unity with all Mankind. Though born in an orthodox family, his piousness was balanced by an unusual broadmindedness and lack of prejudice.

Sivananda's passion for service drew him to a medical career, and he gravitated to those parts of the world that most needed his services. He established a distinguished practice in Malaysia. He also edited a health journal and wrote extensively on health problems. He discovered that people needed right knowledge most of all. Dissemination of that knowledge he espoused as his own mission.

It was divine dispensation, and the blessing of God upon Mankind that this doctor of body and mind renounced his career and took to a life of renunciation in order to minister to the souls of people. He settled down in Rishikesh in 1924, practiced intense austerities and shone as a great Yogi, saint, sage, and liberated soul.

In 1932 he started the Sivanandashram, and in 1936 the Divine Life Society was born.The Yoga Vedanta Forest Academy was organized in 1948. Dissemination of spiritual knowledge and the training of people in Yoga and Vedanta was their aim and function. Sivananda is the author of over two hundred books, and has disciples all over the world, belonging to all nationalities, religions, and creeds. He entered Mahasamadhi in 1963.

Music is Gandharva Vidya. It is the most ancient of arts. ~
pitiated Lord Siva through music. Music is the medium for ~
emotion. Music kindles love and infuses hope. It has countless v~
instruments. Music is in the hearts of all men and women. Mus~ is on
their tongues.

NATURE'S MUSIC

Music is in the winds and the waves. Music is in the nightingale. It is
in the cinema-stars and musicians. It is in the concert, orchestra and the-
atres. There is music in the running brooks. There is music in the cry of
children. There is music in all things, if you have ears.

THE POWER OF MUSIC

Sound is the first manifestation of the Absolute. Supercharged with transcendent soul-force, sound is, in all creation, the one powerful principle
that widely influences and effectively brings under control all other manifestations. Many examples can be quoted to bear testimony to this claim
of sound with reference to both the individual and the cosmos.

We have heard how Tansen was able to make it rain through the Megha
Raga, how he lighted the lamp through singing in Dipaka Raga. There are,
again, certain accounts relating to the Tibetan Lamas, which tell us how the
Lamas drove away and dispersed rain-bearing clouds, or gathered the
clouds and made them rain by blowing the horns and the trumpets and
beating the drums. We have also heard how the deer is entrapped by sweet
sound, how the cobra is enchanted by sweet music. Raga Punnagavarali
charms the cobra. Nada entraps the mind. The mind gets Laya in sweet
Nada.

Mark the power of gentle, sweet sounds: Sa, Ri, Ga, Ma, Pa, Dha, Ni,
Sa. Music has charms to soothe a ferocious tiger. It melts rocks and bends
the banyan tree. It enraptures, lulls, and energises. It elevates, inspires,
strengthens, and invigorates. It vibrates in the memory. It cures incurable
diseases. Music fills the mind with Sattva. Music generates harmony in the
heart. Music melts the hardest heart. Music softens the brutal nature of
man. Music comforts, soothes and cheers up people when they are afflicted. It comforts the lonely and the distressed. Music removes worries,
cares and anxieties. It makes you forget the world. Man wants music to
relax and elevate him.

The devotee sits with his Ektar Tambura to melt his mind in his Lord in
silence. Narada Rishi roams about in the three worlds with his Tambura in
his hand, singing Sriman Narayana Narayana. Music helps the devotee to
commune with the Lord. It makes the mind one-pointed quickly. Music
brings Bhava Samadhi. Thyagaraja, Purandara Das, Mira, and Tukaram
have all realised God through music.

PRANAVA - THE SOURCE OF ALL MUSIC

Wherefrom has music derived this mighty power? From the supreme
music of Brahman, the sacred Pranava. Listen to the vibration of the Tambura or the Veena: do you hear the majestic Pranava-Nada? All the musical notes are blended beautifully into this Pranava. All the musical notes
spring from this Pranava. Music is intended to reverberate this Pranava-
Nada in your heart. For, Om or the Pranava is your real name, your real

Svarupa. Therefore you love to hear music, which is but the most melodious intonation of your own essential name. When the mind thus gets attracted, and gets unified with one's essential nature, the great power of God stored up there wells up within and heals body and mind.

BHAVA SAMADHI AND SUPER INTUITIONAL KNOWLEDGE

He who does Sangita forgets the body and the world. Sangita removes Dehadhyasa or identification with the body. The Bhakta enters into Bhava Samadhi by singing devotional music. He comes face to face with the greatest storehouse of knowledge and wisdom, Ananda or Supreme Bliss. Therefore he emerges from this Samadhi as a Jnani, and radiates peace, bliss and wisdom all around.

Tukaram was an agricultural peasant. He could not even sign his name. He was always doing Sankirtan of Lord Krishna's Name Vitthala, Vitthala with cymbals in his hands. He had Darshana of Lord Krishna in physical form. His inner sight or Divya Drishti was opened by Sankirtan. His inspiring Abhangas are texts for M.A. students of the Bombay University. Wherefrom did the unlettered Tuka derive his knowledge? He tapped the fountain of knowledge through Sankirtan. He penetrated into the divine source through Bhava Samadhi that was brought about by deep Sankirtan.

MUSIC IS SPIRITUAL

Music is not an instrument for titillation of the nerves or satisfaction of the senses; it is a Yoga Sadhana which enables you to attain Atma-sakshatkara. It is the foremost duty of all musicians, and institutions interested in the promotion of music, to preserve this grand ideal and this pristine purity that belong to music.

Saint Thyagaraja, Purandara Das, and others have repeatedly pointed this out; and by their own life renunciation and devotion they have emphasized that music should be treated as Yoga, and that true music can be tasted only by one who has freed himself from all taints of worldliness, and who practises music as a Sadhana for Self-realisation. Thyagaraja was a devotee of Lord Rama. Most of his devotional songs are in praise of Lord Rama. He had direct Darshana of Lord Rama on several occasions. Purandara Das worshipped Lord Vithala, and spent forty years in the dissemination of Bhakti all over the land through his songs. He heard the music of the soul inside, and so he gave his thrilling music outside. Mira came face to face with Krishna. She talked with Krishna, her beloved. She drank the Krishna - prema-rasa. She has sung from the core of her heart the music of her soul, the music of her beloved, her unique spiritual experiences. Her language of love is so powerful that even a downright atheist will be moved by her devotional songs. Syama Sastrigal was a great devotee of Devi. He enjoyed the abundant grace of mother Kamakshi. Muthuswami Dikshitar, the great Nada Jyotis, regarded Lord Subrahmanya Himself as his Supreme Guru, and all his compositions bear the Mudra GURU-GUHA.

Music is Nada Yoga. The various musical notes have their own corresponding Nadis or subtle channels in the Kundalini Chakras; and music vibrates these Nadis, purifies them, and awakens the psychic and spiritual power dormant in them. Purification of Nadis not only ensures peace and happiness of mind, but goes a long way in Yoga Sadhana and helps the aspirant to reach the goal of life very easily.

INFLUENCE OF MUSIC OVER MIND AND BODY

Sweet melody exercises a powerful influence on the mind and physical nature of every living being. Trapped in music, the mysterious mind with its thousand hoods of Vasanas and Vrittis, lies quiescently on the lap of the Sadhaka; and he can make it dance to his tune, control it according to his will, and mould it as he pleases. Mind, the instrument of Satan in man, the magic-wand of Maya, the terror of all spiritual aspirants, is there in the hands of this Music Yogi under his perfect control. The wonder of wonders in the case of this Music Yoga is that it is not only the mind of the musician which is thus controlled, but the minds of all those who listen to the music. They become calm, peaceful, and blissful. That is why great saints like Mira Bai, Tukaram, Kabir Das, Sri Thyagaraja, Purandara Das and others wove their Upadesha into sweet music; with the sweet music, these sublime thoughts would easily get into the heart of the listener, which is at other times zealously guarded by the vicious cobra of worldliness.

The Rishis of yore have invariably written their inspiring works either in the form of poetry or in the form of songs. Our scriptures - the Vedas, Smritis, Puranas etc. - are all set to music, and are metrical compositions. There is rhythm, metre and melody in them. Sama Veda, especially is unrivalled in its music.

Music is an aid to treatment of diseases. Sages affirm that many diseases can be cured by the melodious sound of a flute or a violin, a Veena or a Sarangi. They maintain that there is, in music, an extraordinary power over diseases. Harmonious rhythm caused by sweet music has attractive property. It draws out disease. The disease comes out to encounter the music wave. The two blend together and vanish in space.

Music relaxes nervous tension, and makes parts of the body affected by tension to resume their normal functions. In America, doctors are treating patients who are suffering from nervous diseases through music. In ancient Egypt, music was used in temples in healing diseases of the nervous class.

Sangita or Kirtan is the best medicine and tonic when all other systems of medicine have failed to cure a disease. Kirtan will work wonders. Kirtan is the sole refuge and sheet-anchor in the treatment of chronic incurable diseases. Try this unique medicine and realise its marvellous benefits. If anyone is suffering from any disease, do Kirtan near his bed. He will soon be cured of his disease.

KIRTANA BHAKTI

Kirtan is singing of the Lord's glories. The devotee is thrilled with divine emotion. He loses himself in the love of God. He gets horripilation in the body due to extreme love for God. He weeps in the middle when thinking of the glory of God. His voice becomes choked, and he flies into a state of divine Bhava.

Kirtan is singing God's name with feeling, love and faith. In Sankirtan, people join together and sing God's Name collectively in a common place. There is accompaniment of musical instruments such as harmonium , violin, cymbals, Mridanga or Khol, etc. Christians sing hymns in the church with piano. This is only Sankirtan. Kirtan is one of the nine modes of Bhakti. Sankirtan is an exact science. One can realize God through Kirtan alone. This is the easiest method for attainment of God-consciousness. Great divine persons like Narada, Valmiki and Suka in ancient times, and Gouranga, Nanak, Tulasidas, Suradas, etc., in comparatively recent times, have all attained perfection through Kirtana Bhakti alone.

The harmonious vibrations produced by the singing of the Names of the Lord help the devotees to control their mind easily. They produce a benign influence on their mind. They elevate the mind at once from its old ruts or grooves to magnanimous heights of divine splendour and glory. If one does Sankirtan from the bottom of his heart with full Bhava and Prem, even the trees, birds and animals will be deeply influenced. They will respond. Such is the powerful influence of Sankirtan.

THE PSYCHOLOGY BEHIND KIRTANA BHAKTI

Kirtana is a very effective method of devotion for another reason. Man is an erotic being. He loves and loves. He cannot but love things of the world; but, his love is only passion and is not pure divine love. He wants to hear sweet music, wants to see beautiful objects, and wants to witness a dance. Music melts the heart of even the stone-hearted man. If at all there is anything in this world which can change the heart of a man in a very quick time, that is music and dance. This very method is made use of in Kirtana Bhakti; but, it is directed towards God instead of towards sensual enjoyments. Man's emotion of erotism is directed towards Divinity, and his love for music and singing is not destroyed; because, sudden destruction of such a sentiment which he holds as very dear will not prove successful in making him perfect. Kirtana is sweet and pleasant, and easily changes the heart.

Kirtana is the most suitable method even for householders. This gives pleasure to the mind, and at the same time, purifies the heart. This has a double effect.

Do Sankirtan daily. Disseminate Sankirtan Bhakti far and wide. Develop Visva-prem through Sankirtan. Establish Sankirtan Mandalis everywhere. Bring Vaikuntha on earth - in every house - by doing Sankirtan! Realise your Sat-Chid-Ananda state!

(From Bliss Divine by Master Sivananda)

Bhakti is resting on God. Bhakti is flow of devotion like the flow of a river. Bhakti is continuity of devotion, just as there is continuity in the flow of oil from one vessel to another vessel. Bhakti is attraction of the Jiva to the Lord, just as there is attraction of the needle to the magnet.

Bhakti is love for love's sake. The devotee wants God and God alone. There is no selfish expectation here. There is no fear also. Is the son afraid of his father who is a Sessions Judge? Is the wife afraid of her husband? So also, a devotee entertains the least fear of God. The fear of-retribution vanishes in him. He feels, believes, conceives, and imagines that his Ishtam is an ocean of love or Prem. Bhakti transmutes man into Divinity. It intoxicates the devotee with divine Prem. It gives him eternal satisfaction. It makes him perfect. It weans the mind from sensual objects. It makes him rejoice in God. Emotional excitement is not devotion to God. Devotion is pure love. Fanaticism is not devotion. It is frenzy. It is mere excitement. Bhakti is not mere emotionalism, but is the tuning of the will as well as the intellect towards the Divine. It is supreme love of God. It blossoms afterwards into Jnana. It leads to immortality or God-realization. Bhakti is the direct approach to the ideal through the heart. Love is natural to everybody.

BHAKTI IS OPEN TO ALL

Bhakti can be practised under all conditions and by all alike. Learning, austere penance, study of the Vedas, and brilliant intellect are not needed for the attainment of Bhakti or devotion. What is wanted is constant and living remembrance of God, coupled with faith. That is the reason why the path of Bhakti is available for everyone.

Nishada was born in a low caste; Sabari was a rustic woman; Dhruva was an uneducated boy; Vidura and Sudama were very poor; Vibhishana was an ugly Rakshasa; Hanuman was a monkey; Jatayu was a bird; Gajendra was an elephant; the Gopis of Brindavan were not initiated into Vedic rites; but all these attained God-realisation on account of their devotion and self-surrender.

THE EASIEST APPROACH TO GOD

Bhakti is easier than any other way of approach to God. In Jnana and Yoga, there is the risk of a fall. In the path of devotion, there is no risk as the devotee receives full support and help from God. Those who tread the path of Jnana and Yoga are liable to become proud of their powers and wisdom. Bhaktas are humble. Humility is the foundation of Bhakti Yoga. Jnana Yoga is the Yoga of wisdom. It is the path of analysis and rejection. It is the path of endless negation. This is a very difficult path. Raja Yoga also is difficult. It is like stilling the waves of the ocean. You will have to still all the thought waves. Karma Yoga also is difficult. It is like climbing to the highest peak. You need tremendous will power. Bhakti Yoga alone is easy. The Lord is stretching His hands to lift you up from the mire of Samsara. You will have to grasp His hand firmly. But, one thing is absolutely essential here. You should not have any other thought than that of God and God alone.

ONE-POINTEDNESS IN DEVOTION

The child thinks of the mother and mother alone. A passionate husband thinks of his wife and wife alone. A greedy man thinks of his money and money alone. Even so, the devotee should entertain in his heart the picture of his Ishtam and Ishtam alone. Then he can have Darshan of God easily.

Objects are enemies of God. Sons, wife, property, cattle, houses, friends, and relatives are enemies of God. You must cherish perfect indifference to these objects. You must not think of the body and its wants too much. Thoughts of body, thoughts of food, thoughts of wife and children make you forget God. You cannot have thoughts of God if you have thoughts of Anatma things. If the devotee loves God sometimes and his wife, son, money, house, cattle, and property also at other times, it is Vyabhicharini Bhakti. The love is divided. A small portion of the mind is given to God. The remaining portion is given to family and possessions.

The Lord becomes the slave of a Bhakta only when the latter has made absolute, ungrudging self-surrender. The Lord is very cruel and puts His devotees to severe tests and trials. He did not hear the words of Draupadi so long as she kept up her own strength and traces of egoism. When she cried aloud with perfect sincerity and total resignation, "O Dwarakanath, my Beloved! Come to my rescue", then He ran to the scene, and she had abundant cloth and her modesty was saved.

Generally the aspirant, consciously or unconsciously, wittingly or unwittingly, keeps up some desires for his gratification. He does not wish to part completely with his desires. Therefore the self-surrender does not become perfect and unreserved. So the grace of the Lord does not descend. Even if there is an atom of desire or egoism, there is no possibility of divine grace.

DEVOTION AND DESIRE

Desire obstructs the growth of devotion. Devotion to the Lord increases in intensity when mundane desires are renounced. Renunciation is the very essence of devotional love. Divine love has no element of desire in it. Devotion cannot co-exist with desire of any kind, not even the desire for Liberation. The devotee wants God and God alone, and His service. The devotee loves God and serves Him and His creation. He does not strive consciously for Mukti, but God confers Mukti on His devotee unsolicited.

HOW TO CULTIVATE DEVOTION

People put a question: "How can we love God whom we have not seen?" Live in the company of saints. Hear the Lilas of God. Study the sacred scriptures. Worship Him first in His several forms as manifested in the world. Worship any image or picture of the Lord or the Guru. Recite His Name. Sing His glories. Stay for one year in Ayodhya or Brindavan, Chitrakuta or Pandharpur, Benares or Ananda Kutir. You will develop love for God. Every act must be done that awakens the emotion of Bhakti. Keep the Puja room clean. Decorate the room. Burn incense. Light a lamp. Keep a clean seat. Bathe. Wear clean clothes. Apply Vibhuti or Bhasma, and Kumkum on the forehead. Wear Rudraksha or Tulsi Mala. All these produce a benign influence on the mind and elevate the mind. They generate piety. They help to create the necessary Bhava or feeling to invoke the Deity that you want to worship. The mind will be easily concentrated.

Practice of right conduct, satsanga, japa, smarana, kirtan, prayer, worship, service of saints, residence in places of pilgrimage, service of the poor and the sick with divine Bhava, observance of Varnashrama duties, offering of all actions and their fruits to the Lord, feeling the presence of the Lord in all beings, prostrations before the image and saints, renunciation of earthly enjoyments and wealth, charity, austerities and vows, practice of Ahimsa, Satyam, and Brahmacharya - all these will help you to develop Bhakti.

BHAVAS IN BHAKTI YOGA

There are six kinds of Bhavas in Bhakti. In Shanta Bhava, the devotee is Shanta or peaceful. He does not jump and dance. He is not highly emotional. His heart is filled with love and joy. Bhishma was a Shanta Bhakta. Sri Hanuman was a Dasya Bhakta. He had Dasya Bhava. He served Lord Rama whole-heartedly. He pleased his master in all possible ways. He found joy and bliss in the service of his Master.

In Sakhya Bhava, God is a friend of the devotee. Arjuna had this Bhava towards Lord Krishna. The devotee moves with the Lord on equal terms. Arjuna and Krishna used to sit, eat, talk and walk together as intimate friends. In Vatsalya Bhava, the devotee looks upon God as his child. Yasoda had this Bhava with Lord Krishna. There is no fear in this Bhava, because God is your pet child. The devotee serves, feeds and looks upon God as a mother does in the case of her child. The fifth Bhava is Sakhya Bhava. This is also known as Gopi Bhava. The Gopis united Radha and Krishna when they separated. They identified themselves with Radha and Krishna and enjoyed the bliss resulting from their reunion.

The last is Madhurya Bhava or Kanta Bhava. This is the highest form of Bhakti. This was the relation between Radha and Krishna. This is Atmasamarpana. The lover and the beloved become one. The devotee and God feel one with each other and still maintain a separateness in order to enjoy the bliss of the play of love between them. This is oneness in separation and separation in oneness. The relationship is that of husband and wife. Jayadeva, Mira and Andal has this Bhava.

APARA BHAKTI AND PARA BHAKTI

Bhakti is of two kinds, Apara Bhakti and Para Bhakti. Apara Bhakti is lower Bhakti. In Apara Bhakti, the devotee is a neophyte. He observes rituals and ceremonies. He has no expanded heart. He is a sectarian. He dislikes other kinds of Bhaktas who worship other Devatas.

A devotee of Para Bhakti type is all-embracing and all-inclusive. He has cosmic love or Visvaprem. The whole world is Brindavan for him. He does not visit temples for worship. He sees the Lord in everything. He feels that the world is a manifestation of the Lord, and all movements and actions are his Lila. He has no Ghrina or dislike for faecal matter or dirt, for the Chandala, the scavenger, the cobbler, the beggar, the prostitute, or the thief. He says, "I see everywhere my sweet Lord. It is Hari who is playing the part of the prostitute, the thief, the dacoit, the scavenger!". He has an all-embracing, all inclusive, exalted mental state. This cannot be adequately described in words. It has to be felt. Mira, Gouranga, Hafiz, Tulsidas, Kabir, Ramdas - all enjoyed this state.

Namdev said to the dog: "O Vittala, my dear, in the form of a dog, do not run away with the dry bread. It will affect your soft throat. Pray let me apply ghee to the bread". He ran with ghee in a cup to the dog. Sri Ramakrishna Paramahamsa prostrated before an outcaste girl: "O Mother Kali! I see Thee in this girl". Eknath, a Maharashtrian Bhakta, gave his ring voluntarily to the thief when the latter entered the house: "O thief! Take this ring also. Your duty is to steal things. Thou art Krishna. Keep up this Lila". Have you understood the sublime state of these exalted Bhaktas who have a new angle of vision? A day will come to you also. Exert. Struggle.

PARA BHAKTI AND JNANA

Para Bhakti is Jnana only. Para Bhakti and Jnana are one. Sri Sankara, a Kevala - advaita-jnani, was a great Bhakta of Lord Hari, Hara and Devi. Sri Ramakrishna Paramahamsa worshipped Kali and got Jnana through Swami Totapuri, his Advaita Guru. Appayya Dikshitar, famous Jnani of South India, was a devout Bhakta of Lord Siva. Para Bhakti and Jnana are one. The only slight difference is: a Bhakta uses his emotion; a Jnani uses his will and intellect. Bhakti begins with love, and Jnana with thinking and self-analysis. The end of both is the same, union with the Divine. A devotee contracts. A Vedantin expands. The former contracts and enters the Lord through self-surrender. The latter expands and becomes one with Brahman through assertion and identification.

The fruit of Bhakti is Jnana. Jnana intensifies Bhakti. Even Jnanis like Sankara, Madhusudana, and Suka Deva took to Bhakti after Realisation to enjoy the sweetness of loving relationship with God. Knowledge or wisdom will dawn by itself when you practise Bhakti Yoga. Bhakti is the pleasant, smooth, direct road to God. Bhakti is sweet in the beginning, in the middle and in the end. It gives the highest, undecaying bliss. Kindle love divine in thy heart, for this is the immediate way to the Kingdom of God. Pray to the Lord. Sing his glory. Recite His name. Become a channel of His grace. Seek His will. Do his will. Surrender to His will. You will become one with the cosmic will.

Surrender unto the Lord. He will become your charioteer on the field of life. He will drive your chariot well. You will reach the destination, the Abode of Immortal Bliss.

(From Bliss Divine by Master Sivananda)

JAYA GANESHA   RAGA - Kalyan   TAL - Keherwa

OM OM OM
1. JAYA GANESHA JAYA GANESHA JAYA GANESHA PAHI MAAM
   SREE GANESHA SREE GANESHA SREE GANESHA RAKSHA
   MAAM
   SARAVANABHAVA SARAVANABHAVA SARAVANABHAVA PAHI MAAM
   SUBRAMANYA SUBRAMANYA SUBRAMANYA RAKSHA MAAM

2. JAYA SARASWATEE JAYA SARASWATEE JAYA SARASWATEE PAHI MAAM
   SREE SARASWATEE SREE SARASWATEE SREE SARASWATEE RAKSHA MAAM

3. JAYA GURU SHIVA GURU HARE GURU RAAM
   JAGAT GURU PARAM GURU SAT GURU SHYAAM

4. OM AADI GURU ADWAITA GURU AANANDA GURU OM
   CHID GURU CHIDGANA GURU CHINMAYA GURU OM

5. HARE RAAMA HARE RAAMA RAAMA RAAMA HARE HARE
   HARE KRISHNA HARE KRISHNA KRISHNA KRISHNA HARE HARE

6. OM NAMAH SHIVAAYA OM NAMAH SHIVAAYA
   OM NAMAH SHIVAAYA OM NAMAH SHIVAAYA

7. OM NAMO NAARAAYANAAYA OM NAMO NARAAYANAAYA
   OM NAMO NAARAAYANAAYA OM NAMO NARAAYANAAYA

8. OM NAMO BHAGAVATE VASUDEVAAYA
   OM NAMO BHAGAVATE VASUDEVAAYA

9. OM NAMO BHAGAVATE SHIVAANANDAYA
   OM NAMO BHAGAVATE SAT GURU NAATHAAYA

10. OM NAMO BHAGAVATE VISHNU DEVAANANDAAYA
    OM NAMO BHAGAVATE VISHNU DEVAANANDAAYA

11. SREE RAAM JAYA RAAM JAYA JAYA RAAM OM
    SREE RAAM JAYA RAAM JAYA JAYA RAAM OM

12. KRISHNAM VANDE JAGAT GURUM
    SHRI KRISHNAM VANDE JAGAT GURUM

13. AANANDOHAM AANANDOHAM AANANDAM BRAHM AANANDAM
    OM NAMAH SHIVAAYA OM NAMAH SHIVAAYA

JAYA GANESHA MEANING

These Mantras are arranged in a logical and traditional sequence. They are chanted in the beginning of Satsang to create a pure Satwick atmosphere.

1   "Jaya" means "hail" or "victory to";
Ganesha is first invoked to remove all obstacles on the physical, mental and astral planes.
Pahimaam means "save me", and Rakshamaam means "protect me".

2. Saravanabhava (or Subramanya, Kartikeya, Shanmuga, or Murugan as he is also known) is the leader of the army of the gods whose job is to destroy all demons. Lord Saravanabhava drives off all evil influcences (lust, anger, greed, etc.). He insures victory in both the inner and the outer battle.

3. Saraswati is the Godess of the Arts and Wisdom. Invoking her name gives intelligence, self-control, ability and success in deep study and scholarly projects, bestows increased intuition, mystical and academic wisdom.

4. Next the Guru is saluted. We see him as the personification and transmitter of the teachings of God in the form of Siva, Hari and Rama. He is the World (Jagad) teacher, the highest (Param) Guru, who lives the truth (Sad) and bestows auspiciousness (Shyam). In short, we see the Guru as God. He is the beginningless (Adi) One (Advaita - without a second) Guru, the bestower of Bliss (Ananda), Knowledge Absolute (Chid, Chidgana), and the vanquisher of Maya (Chinmaya).
Knowledge is transmitted from the teacher to the student. Everyone should accept a teacher and remember that it is not actually important whether the teacher is well-known or little-known, but it is the disciple's faith in the Guru that is important. Spiritual knowledge is transmitted from Guru to Disciple. When a student accepts a teacher, he is also implicitly accepting the Master of his teacher as he will be inheriting the spiritual wealth of both. The disciple, in turn, passes on his wealth, and thus, spiritual inheritance is continued.

5. This is known as "Maha Mantra" meaning "Great Mantra". It is said to be the most powerful one in this Iron Age (Kali Yuga). This Mantra should always be sung in its entirety and not broken in any way. This Mantra can be chanted to help bring about peace in the world.

6. This is the Mantra of Lord Siva, the primordial Yogi. This Mantra destroys all negative tendencies and bestows physical and mental poise, intuitive knowledge, integratsicion of mind and intellect, great strength in spiritual practices. Protects one from the effects of past bad Karma.

7. The Mantra of Lord Vishnu (Narayana) is chanted to invoke His all-pervading power of mercy and goodness. It is through His Grace that Righteousness is able to prevail. Repetition of this Mantra confers infinite love, prosperity, power, glory, wisdom and total liberation. Gives the ability to dissolve obstacles resulting from egoism and ignorance.This mantra is chanted for World Peace and inner harmony.

8. The Mantra of Krishna (also called Vasudeva) is chanted to remind us of all His wonderful teachings, as bestower of the Bhagavad Gita on mankind. Grants enjoyments as well as spiritual realization. Gives success in all undertakings.

9. Salutations to the Divine Sivananda, the Divine Sadguru, our Master

10. Salutations to Swami Vishnu Devananda our Guru.

11. Salutations to Rama, the seventh incarnation of Vishnu, the incarnation of righteousness and Divine conduct.

12. Again, Krishna is addressed as the World (Jagad) teacher (Guru). Here we thank Him (Vande) and say "It is to thee that we owe all Knowledge."

13. Culminating in the expression and affirmation that "I am Bliss, Bliss absolute. The student of Vedanta always strive to identify with his Divine Self, the Atman or Soul which is of the nature of Absolute Bliss.

PREMA MUDITA MANASE KAHO

RAGA - Bhairavi   TAL - Dadra

1   PREMA MUDITA MANASAY KAHO
     RAAMA RAAMA RAAM
     SREE RAAMA RAAM RAAM

2   PAAPA KAATAY DUHKA MITAY LEKE RAAM NAAM
     BHAVASAMUDRA SUKHADA NAAVA
     EK RAAMA NAAM   (SREE RAAM RAAM....)

3   PARAMA SHAANTI SUKHANIDHAANA DIVYA RAAMA NAAM
     NIRAADHARAAKO ADHAARA
     EK RAAMA NAAM   (SREE RAAM RAAM....)

4   PARAMA GOPYA PARAMA ISHTA MANTRA RAAM NAAM
     SANTA HRIDAYA SADAA VASATA
     EK RAAMA NAAM   (SREE RAAM RAAM...)

5   MAHAA DEVA SATATA JAPATA DIVYA RAAMA NAAM
     KAASHEE MARATA MUKTI KARATA
     KAHATA RAAMA NAAM   (SREE RAAM RAAM...)

6   MAATAA PITAA BANDHU SAKHAA SABAHI RAAMA NAAM
     BHAKTA JANANA JEEVANADHANA
     EK RAAMA NAAM   (SREE RAAM RAAM....)

MEANING

1   Repeat the name "Rama" with a mind filled with love and joy.

2   By repeating the name, sins and miseries are extinguished.
The name of Rama is the only boat to cross the ocean of Samsara.

3   The Divine Name Rama is the abode of supreme peace and bliss.
Rama Nam is the only support of the supportless.

4   Rama Nam is the most sacred and fruitful Mantra.
Rama Nam ever dwells in the hearts of sages.

5   Mahadeva (Lord Siva) always chants the Divine Name "Rama".
Lord Siva grants liberation to men who repeat Lord's Name
at the time of death in Kashi (Benares).

6   Rama Nam is mother, father, relative, friend, all in all.
Rama Nam is the life treasure of the devotees.

AADI DIVYA

RAGA - Bhairavi   **TAL - Dadra**

AADI DIVYA JYOTI MAHAA
KAALI MAA NAMAH
MADHUSHUMBHAMAHISHAMARDINEE
MAHAA SHAKTAYAY NAMAH
BRAHMAA VISHNU SHIVA SWAROOPA
TWAM NAA ANYATHAA
CHARAA CHARASYA PAALIKAA
NAMO NAMAH SADAA

MEANING

Salutations to Great Mother Kali
Who art the first (light) exploding in the Universe.
We prostrate to Thee,
the great power and destroyer of the demons,
Madhu, Shumbha and Mahish, (our lower nature).
Thou art nothing but of the nature of Brahma, Vishnu, and Siva.
We prostrate always to Thee,
Oh Protector of the Universe.

LINGAAHSTAKAM   (Eight verses on Lord Siva)

RAGA - Bhupali   TAL - Keherwa

1   BRAHMAMURAARISURARCHITALINGAM
    NIRMALABHAASHITASHOBHITALINGAM
    JANMAJADUHKHAVINASHAKALINGAM
    TATPRANAMAAMI SADAASHIVALINGAM

2   DEVAMUNIPRAVARAARCHITALINGAM
    KAAMADAHAM KARUNAKARALINGAM
    RAAVANADARPAVINAASHANALINGAM
    TATPRANAMAAMI.......

3   SARVASUGANDHASULEPITALINGAM
    BUDDHIVIVARDHANAKAARANALIGAM
    SIDDHASURAASURAVANDITALINGAM
    TATPRANAMAAMI.....

4   KANAKAMAHAAMANIBHOOSHITALINGAM
    PHANIPATIVESHTITASHOBHITALINGAM
    DAKSHASUYAJNAVINAASHANALIGAM
    TATPRANAMAAMI...

5   KUNKUMACHANDANALEPITALINGAM
    PANKAJAHAARASUSHOBHITALINGAM
    SANCHITAAPAAPAVINAASHANALINGAM
    TATPRANAMAAMI....

6   DEVAGANAARCHITASEVITALINGAM
    BHAAVAIRBHAKTIBHIREVA CHA LINGAM
    DINAAKARAKOTIPRABHAAKARALINGAM
    TATPRANAMAAMI....

7   ASHTADALOPARIVESHTITALINGAM
    SARVASAMUDBHAVAKAARANALINGAM
    ASHTADARIDRAVINAASHANALINGAM
    TATPRANAMAAMI......

8   SURAGURUSURAVARAPOOJITALINGAM
    SURAVANAPUSHPASADAARCHITALINGAM
    PARAATPARAM PARAMAATMAKALINGAM
    TATPRANAMAAMI......

MEANING

1   Lingam: the symbol of Lord Siva is adored by Brahma, Vishnu and all gods. Taintless, shining, beautiful is Lingam; Destroyer of miseries that follow birth, is Lingam. I salute that Lingam of eternal Siva.

2   The Lingam (symbol) that is adored by the gods and great sages, that denotes the destruction of the god of lust, ocean of mercy, and the vanquishment of Ravana's pride - to that Lingam of the omnipresent Siva I prostrate.

3   The Lingam, that is well anointed with all fragrant materials like sandal paste etc. , the Lingam that enhances the intellect and that is worshipped by Siddhas, gods and Asuras to that Lingam.......

4   The Lingam that is adorned with jewels of gold and precious gems, that shines with the Lord of the serpents that encircles it, and that obstructed the sacrifice performed by Daksha to that Lingam..........

5   The Lingam that is smeared with vermilion and sandal paste, that shines with garlands of lotuses and that dispels all the sins (of devotees) to that Lingam......

6   The Lingam that is adored and worshipped by Gods with great devotional feelings and that shines with brilliance of crores of suns - to that Lingam.....

7   The Lingam that is seated on an eight-petaled seat, that is the cause of all creations and that destroys all eight kinds of destitution - to that Lingam.....

8   The Lingam that is worshipped by the preceptor of gods (Brihaspati) and gods, offering the flowers grown in the heavenly gardens and the Lingam that is the supreme Soul to that Lingam....
(Whoever chants these eight verses in a Siva temple will attain Siva-loka and will rejoice with Lord Siva).

NAAMA RAMAAYANAM

RAGA - Desh   TAL - Kherava

BALAKAANDAM

SHREE RAAM JAYA RAAM JAYA JAYA RAAM (8X)

SHUDDHA BRAHMA PARAATPARA RAAM
KAALAATMAKA PARAMESHWARA RAAM
SESHA KALPA SUKHA NIDRITA RAAM
BRAHMADYAMARA PRARTHITA RAAM
CHANDRA KIRANA KULA MANDANA RAAM
SREEMAD DASARATHA NANDANA RAAM
KAUSALYA SUKHAVARDHANA RAAM
VISHVAAMITRA PRIYADHANA RAAM
GHORA TAATAKA GHAATAKA RAAM

MAAREECHADI NIPAATAKA RAAM
KAUSKIKA MAKHA SAMRAKSHAKA RAAM
SREEMAD AHALYODDHARAKA RAAM
GAUTAMAMUNI SAMPJITA RAAM
SURAMUNIVARAGANA SAMSTUTA RAAM
NAAVIKA DHAAVITA MRIDUPADA RAAM
MITHILAAPURA JANA MOKADA RAAM
VIDEHA MAANASA RANGAKA RAAM
TRYAMBAKA KAARMUKA BHANJAKA RAAM
SEETARPITA VARAMAALIKA RAAM
KRITA VAIVAHIKA KAUTUKA RAAM
BHAARGAVA DARPA VINAASAKA RAAM
SREEMADAYODHAPAALAKA RAAM

SHUDDHA BRAHMA PARATPARA RAAM
KAALAATHMAKA PARAMESHVARA RAAM

AYODHYAKAANDAM

AGANITA GUNAGANA BHOOSHITA RAAM
AVANEETHANAYAA KAAMITA RAAM
RAAKAA CHANDRA SAMAANANA RAAM
PITR VAAKYAASHRITA KAANANA RAAM
PRIYA GUHA VINIVEDITA PADA RAAM
TAKSHAA LITA NIJA MRIDU PADA RAAM
BHARADWAAJA MUKHAANANDAKA RAAM
CHITHRAKOOTAADRI NIKETHANA RAAM
DASHRATHA SANTATA CHINTITA RAAM
KAIKEYEE TANAYARTHITA RAAM
VIRACHITA NIJA PITRI KARMAKA RAAM
BHARATAARPITA NIJAPAADUKA RAAM

ARANYAKAANDAM

DANADAKAAVANA JANAPAAVANA RAAM
DUSHTA VIRAADHA VINAASHANA RAAM
SHARA BHANGA SUTEEKSHNAARCHITA RAAM
AGASTYAANUGRAHA VARHDHITA RAAM
GRIDHRAADHIPA SAMSEVITA RAAM
PANCHAVATEE TATA SUSTHITA RAAM

SHOORPANAKHAARTI VIDHAAYAKA RAAM
KHARADOOSHANA MUKHA SOODAKA RAAM
SEETAPRIYA HARINAANUGA RAAM
MAAREECHAARTI KRIDAASHUGA RAAM
VINASHTA SEETANVESHAKA RAAM
GRIDHRAADHIPA GATHIDAAYAKA RAM

SHABAREE DATTA PHALAASHANA RAAM
KABANDHA BAHOOCHEDANA RAAM

KISKINDHAAKAANDAM

HANUMAT SEVITA NIJAPADA RAAM
NATA SUGREEVAABHEESHTADA RAAM
GARVITA VAALI SAMHAARAKA RAAM
VAANARA DOOTA PRESHAKA RAAM

HITAKARA LAKSHAMANA SANYUTHA RAAM
KAPIVARA SANTATA SAMSMRITA RAAM
TAD GATI VIGHNADHVAMSAKA RAAM
SEETA PRAANA DHAARAKA RAAM
DUSHTA DASHAASHANA DOOSHITA RAAM
SHISHTA HANUMAT BHOOSHITA RAAM

SEETA VEDITA KAAKAAVANA RAAM
KRITA CHOODAMANI DARSHANA RAAM
KAPIVARA VACHANAASHVAASITA RAAM

YUDDHAKAANDAM

RAAVANA NIDHANA PRASTHITA RAAM
VAANARA SAINYA SAMAAVRITA RAAM
SOSHITA SARIDEE SHAARTHITA RAAM

VIBHEESHANAA BHAYA DAAYAKA RAAM
PARVATHA SETU NIBANDHAKA RAAM
KUMBHAKARNA SHIRASCHEDAKA RAAM
RAAKSHASA KOTI VIMARDAKA RAAM
AHIMAHI RAAVANA MARANA RAAM
SAMHRITHA DASHAMUKHA RAAVANA RAAM

VIDHI BHAVA MUKHA SURA SAMSTUTA RAAM

SVASTHITA DASHARATHA VEKSHITA RAAM
SEETAA DARSHANA MODITA RAAM
ABHISHIKTA VIBHEESHANANGATA RAAM
PUSHPAKA YAANAAROHANA RAAM
BHARADVAJADI NISHEVANA RAAM

BHARATA PRAANA VITHARANA RAAM
SAKETAPUREE BHOOSHANA RAAM
SAKALA SVEEYA SAMANANA RAAM
RATNA LASAT PEETHASTHITA RAAM
PATTABHISHEKALAMKRITHA RAAM
PARTHIVA KULASAMAANITA RAAM

VIBHEESHANARPITA RANJAKA RAAM
KEESHA KULAANUGRAHAKARA RAM
SAKALA JEEVA SAMRAKSHAKA RAAM
SAMASTA LOKAA DHAARAKA RAAM
RAMA RAMA JAYA RAJA RAAM
RAMA RAMA JAYA SEETAA RAAM
SHREE RAAM JAYA RAAM JAYA JAYA RAAM (8X)

(ADDENDUM) UTTARAKAANDAM

AAGATAMUNIGANA SAMSTUTA RAAM
VISRUTA DASAKANTHODBHAVA RAAM
SITAALINGANA NIRVRITA RAAM
NEETI SURAKSITA JANAPADA RAAM
VIPINATYAJITA JANAKAJA RAAM
KAARITA LAVANASURAVADHA RAAM

SVARGATA SHAMBUKA SAMSTUTA RAAM
SVATANAYA KUSHALAVA NANDITA RAAM
ASVAMEDHA KRATU DIKSITA RAAM
KALAVEDITA SURAPADA RAAM
AYODHYAKA JANA MUKTIDA RAAM
VIDHIMUKHA VIBUDHAANANDAKA RAAM

TEJOMAYA NIJAROOPAKA RAAM
SAMSRITBANDHA VIMOCHAKA RAAM
DHARMASTHAAPANA TATPARA RAAM
BHAKTIPARAYANA MUKTIDA RAAM
SARVA CHARACHARA PAALAKA RAAM
SARVA BHAVAAMAYA VAARAKA RAAM

VAIKUNTHAALAYA SAMSTHITA RAAM
NITYAANANDA PADASTHITA RAAM
RAMA RAMA JAYA RAJA RAAM
RAMA RAMA JAYA SEETAA RAAM

MEANING

BALAKANDAM

O Rama, Thou who art pure Brahman and the greatest of all beings.

O Rama, Thou who art of the nature of Time, and the supreme ruler.

O Rama, Thou who dost slumber on the serpent bed of Sesha.

O Rama, Thou who wert prayed to by Brahma and other gods.

O Rama, Thou who wert an ornament to the solar dynasty.

O Rama, Thou who wert born as the son of Dasaratha.

O Rama, Thou who didst enhance the joy of Thy mother, Kausalya.

O Rama, Thou whom the sage Viswamitra cherished as his most precious wealth.

O Rama, Thou who didst destroy the fierce demoness Tataka.

O Rama, Thou who didst put down the Rakshasas like Maricha.

O Rama, Thou who didst protect the sacrificial rites of Kausika (from the disturbances of Rakshasas).

O Rama, Thou who didst resurrect Ahalya.

O Rama, Thou who wert worshipped by the sage Gautama.

O Rama, Thou who wert praised by the gods and the galaxy of great sages.

O Rama, Thou whose tender feet were washed and worshipped by the boatman.

O Rama, Thou who didst fill the citizens of Mithila with wonder.

O Rama, Thou who didst delight Janaka, the king of Videha.

O Rama, Thou who didst break the bow of Trymbaka (Siva).

O Rama, Thou on whom Sita put her wedding garland.

O Rama, Thou who didst shine in the splendour of the marriage ceremony.

O Rama, Thou who didst humble the pride of Bhargava.

O Rama, Thou who didst look after the government of Ayodhya.

O Rama, Thou who art pure Brahman and the greatest of all beings.

O Rama, Thou who art of the nature of time, and the supreme ruler.

AYODHYAKANDAM

O Rama, Thou who wert possessed of countless virtues.

O Rama, Thou who wert loved by Sita, the daughter of mother earth.

O Rama, Thou whose face was resplendent like the full moon.

O Rama, Thou who didst go to the forest in obedience to Thy father's words.

O Rama, Thou whose feet were worshipped by Thy dear devotee Guha.

O Rama, Thou whose tender feet were washed by him.

O Rama, Thou who didst give great joy to Bharadwaja and others.

O Rama, Thou who didst encamp on Mt. Chitrakuta.

O Rama, Thou who wert the object of constant thought for Dasaratha.

O Rama, Thou who wert supplicated to return by Bharata, the son of Kaikeyi.

O Rama, Thou who didst the obsequies of Thy father Dasaratha.

O Rama, Thou who didst bestow Thy sandals on Bharata.

ARANYAKANDAM

O Rama, Thou who didst sanctify the denizens of the Dandaka forest.

O Rama, Thou who didst destroy the evil demon Viradha.

O Rama, Thou who wert worshipped by the sages Sarabhanga and Sutikshna.

O Rama, Thou who had the blessings of sage Agastya.

O Rama, Thou who wert honoured by the vulture King Jatayu.

O Rama, Thou who didst settle down at Panchavati.

O Rama, Thou who didst punish Surpanakha by mutilation.

O Rama, Thou who destroyed the Asuras headed by Khara and Dushana.

O Rama, Thou who didst chase the deer that fascinated Sita.

O Rama, Thou who by swift arrows terminated Maricha's woes.

O Rama, Thou who didst start in search of the lost Sita.

O Rama, Thou who didst give salvation to Jayatu, the king of vultures.

O Rama, Thou who didst eat the fruit offerings of the woman sage Sabari.

O Rama, Thou who didst cut off the arms of the monster Kabandha.

KISKINDHAKANDAM

O Rama, Thou whose feet were worshipped by Hanumat.

O Rama, Thou who didst fulfill the prayers of Sugriva.

O Rama, Thou who didst kill the proud Bali.

O Rama, Thou who didst send sugriva soldiers on Thy errand.

O Rama, Thou who didst live with Lakshmana as Thy faithful attendant.

SUNDARAKANDAM

O Rama, Thou who wert ever remembered by the sugriva army leader Hanumat.

O Rama, Thou who defeated all obstacles faced by him in his search for Sita.

O Rama, Thou who didst sustain the life of Sita.

O Rama, Thou who wert insulted by the evil Ravana.

O Rama, Thou who wert adored by the noble Hanumat.

O Rama, Thou who wert reminded of the episode of the crow by Sita.

O Rama, Thou who didst behold the crest jewel sent by Sita.

O Rama, Thou who wert consoled by the words of the monkey chief.

YUDDHAKANDAM

O Rama, Thou who didst march forth for the destruction of Ravana.

O Rama, Thou who wert surrounded by the army of sugriva.

O Rama, Thou who wert importuned by the Lord of the seas on Thy threat to dry up the ocean.

O Rama, Thou who didst give refuge to Vibhishana.

O Rama, Thou who didst build with mountains a bridge across the sea.

O Rama, Thou who didst decapitate Kumbhakarna.

O Rama, Thou who didst annihilate the tribe of Rakshasas.

O Rama, Thou who wert spied upon by Ahiravana and Mahiravana in the form of singers.

O Rama, Thou who didst kill Ravana, the extroverted Rakshasa.

O Rama, Thou who wert praised by Brahma, Siva and other gods.

O Rama, Thou whom Dasaratha beheld with joy from his heavenly state.

O Rama, Thou who didst rejoice to see Sita again.

O Rama, Thou who wert worshipped by Vibhishana after his coronation.

O Rama, Thou who didst ascend the aerial vehicle (Pushpaka for returning to Ayodhya).

O Rama, Thou who wert adored by Bharadvaja.

O Rama, Thou who didst fulfil Bharata's expectation (to see Thee return at the stipulated time).

O Rama, Thou who didst become an adornment to the city of Ayodhya.

O Rama, Thou who didst receive the homage of all Thy people.

O Rama, Thou who wert seated on a throne shining with precious stones.

O Rama, Thou who wore the proper robes and decorations for thy coronation.

O Rama, Thou whom all the kings honoured (by offering their obeisance and rich presents).

O Rama, Thou who didst offer to Vibhishna the image of Sri Ranganatha.

O Rama, Thou who didst shower Thy blessings on the hosts of monkeys.

O Rama, Thou who art the protector of all beings.

O Rama, Thou who art the support of all the worlds.

(ADDENDUM) UTTARAKANDAM

O Rama, Thou who wert praised by all the visiting sages.

O Rama, Thou who didst hear about the origin of Ravana.

O Rama, Thou who didst live happily reunited with Sita.

O Rama, Thou who didst establish the rule of law and justice all over the kingdom.

O Rama, Thou who hadst to abandon Sita in the forest.

O Rama, Thou who didst contrive the destruction of Lavanasura.

O Rama, Thou who wert praised by Sambuka to whom Thou didst give salvation.

O Rama, Thou who wert gladdened by the sight of Thy sons Lava and Kusa.

O Rama, Thou who didst perform the Aswamedha sacrifice.

O Rama, Thou who wert reminded of Thy Divine Abode by Kala, the spirit of Time.

O Rama, Thou who didst give salvation to all the inhabitants of Ayodhya.

O Rama, Thou who didst delight Brahma and all the Devas.

O Rama, Thou who didst resume Thy resplendent Divine form.

O Rama, Thou who dost give release from the bondage of repeated births and deaths.

O Rama, Thou who art intent on establishing Dharma.

O Rama, Thou who grantest Mukti (freedom from bondage) to those who are established in Bhakti.

O Rama, Thou who art the protector of all the worlds, sentient and insentient.

O Rama, Thou who dost ward off all the ills of worldly existence.

O Rama, Thou who residest in Thy Abode of Vaikuntha.

O Rama, Thou who art ever established in the state of undecaying Bliss.

O Rama . Hail Rama! Hail Raja Rama!

O Rama. Hail Rama! Hail Sita Rama!

OM JAYA JAGADEESHA HARE

RAGA - Pilu   TAL - Keherwa

1. OM JAYA JAGADEESHA HARE
   SWAAMI JAYA JAGADISHA HARE
   BHAKTA JANON KE SANKATA
   KSHANA ME DOORA KARE
   OM JAYA JAGADISHA HARE.

2. JO DHYAAVE PHALA PAAVE
   DUKHA BINASE MANA KA
   SWAAMEE DUKHA VINASE MANA KA
   SUKHA SAMPATI GHARA AVE

KASHTA MITE TANA KA
OM JAYA JAGADISHA HARE

3. MAATA PITAA TUMA MERE
SHARANA PAROO MAI KISAKI
SWAAMEE SHARANA PAROO MAI KISAKI
TUMA BINA AURA NA DOOJAA
AASHA KAROO MAI KISAKI
OM JAYA JAGADISHA HARE

4. TUMA POORANA PARAMAATMAA
TUMA ANTARAYAAMEE
SWAAMEE TUMA ANTARAYAAMEE
PAARABRAHMA PARAMESWARA
TUMA SABA KE SWAAMEE
OM JAYA JAGADISHA HARE

5. TUMA KARUNAA KE SAGARA
TUMA PAALANAKARATAA
SWAAMEE TUMA PAALANAKARATAA
DEEN DAYAALU KRIPAALU
KRIPA KARO BHARATAA
OM JAYA JAGADISHA HARE

6. TUMA HO EKA AGOCHARA
SAB KEY PRAANAPATI
SWAAMEE SAB KAY PRAANAPATI
KISA VIDHA MILOO DAYAAMAYA
TUMKO MAI KUMATI
OM JAYA JAGADISHA HARE

7. DINA BANDHU DUKHA HARATAA
TUMA RAKSHAKA MERE
SWAAMEE TUMA RAKSHAKA MERE
APANE HAATHA BADHAO
DWAARA PARAA TERE
OM JAYA JAGADISHA HARE

8. VISHAYA VIKAARA MITAAO
PAAPA HARO DEVAA
SWAAMEE PAAPA HARO DEVAA
SRADDHAA BHAKTI BADHAAO
SANTANA KI SEVAA
OM JAYA JAGADISHA HARE

9. JAYA JAGADISHA KI ARAT EE
JO KOI NARA GAAVE
SWAAMEE JO KOI NARA GAVE
KAHATA SIVAANANDA SWAAMEE
SUKHA SAMPATI PAAVE
OM JAYA JAGADISHA HARE

MEANING

1   Salutations and glory to the Lord of the Universe, who is capable of removing the difficulties of devotees instantaneously.

2   He who meditates gains its fruit and miseries of the mind are removed. You can have wealth at your home and pain of the body is destroyed.

3   Thou art my Mother, Thou art my Father.Whom do I surrender myselfto.

4   Thou art perfect God who resides in every soul. Lord of the Universe Thou art the Master of all.

5   Thou art the ocean of compassion nourishing everyone. I am a fool and a villain, living a passionate life. Shower your grace upon me.

6   Thou art one who can not be seen. You are Master of all individualsouls. How can I reach you Oh merciful one, as I am evil minded.

7   Friend of the poor, remover of unhappiness. Thou art my Protector. Raise your hand, as now I have come to Thy door.

8   Please eliminate my desires and passions. Remove my sins. Increase my faith and devotion to serve Holy Men.

9   This body, mind, wealth are all Yours, everything else is also Yours. I am returning all these to You, there is nothing that is mine.Swami Sivananda says, whoever will sing Thy glory in this prayer will find wealth and happiness in his life.

HE PRABHO

1. HE PRABHO AANANDA DAATAA
   JYAANA HAMAKO DIJIYE

2. SHEEGHRA SAARE DURGUNONKO
   DOORA HAMASE KIJIYE

3. LIJIYE HAMAKO SHARANA ME
   HAM SADAACHAAREE BANE

4. BRAHMACHAARI DHARMA RAKSHAKA
   VEERA VRATA DHAAREE BANE

5. HE PRABHO AANANDA DAATAA
   JYHAANA HAMAKO DIJIYE

6. PREMA SE HAMA GURU JANON KEE
   NITYA HI SEVAA KARE

7. SATYA BOLE JHOOTHA TYAAGE
   MELA AAPASA ME KARE

8. HE PRABHO AANANDA DAATAA
   JYNAANA HAMAKO DIJIYE

9. NINDAA KISIKI HAMA KISISE
   BHOOLA KARA BHI NAA KARE

10. DIVYA JEEVANA HO HAMAARAA
    TERE YASHA GAAYAA KARE

    HE PRABHO AANANDA DAATAA
    GYAANA HAMA KO DIJIYE

MEANING

1 O Lord, the giver of bliss bestow on me divine wisdom

2 Quickly take my bad habits very far from me and
   replace them with good ones.

3 Take me who has surrendered unto thee and
   make me one of noble qualities.

4 May the spirituality of Brahmacharya be protected
   Make me an observer of good vows and protector of Dharma.

5 O Lord, Giver of bliss bestow on me divine wisdom

6 May I always serve my Guru with love and devotion.

7 May I always embrace truthfulness and abandon untrouth.

8 O Lord, Giver of bliss,give me knowledge.

9 Help me to never show disrespect to anybody
   and please let me never forget Thee.

10 Let my life be always a divine life and Let me sing thy praises always.

SYMBOLISM OF AARATEE

Lights are waved before the deity. This denotes that the Lord is Jyoti Swarupa. He is Light. The devotee says,"O Lord Thou art the Light in the sun, moon, and fire. Remove the darkness in me by bestowing your Divine Light. May my intellect be illumined." This is the significance of waving lights before the picture of the Lord or before the deities. The names of all the of Gurus from ancient times to present day within our line is repeated and their blessings invoked to bless us with the light of divine knowledge. At the end of the waving of the light, it is taken to the devotes present who symbolically takes the light within himself.

Lighting of camphor denotes that the individual ego should melt like the camphor, and the Jivatman (individual soul) should become one with the Supreme Light of Lights.

Prasad (consecrated food) is offered. The benefits of Prasad are beyond description. They have the power to change the outlook of a person entirely. Prasad and Charanamrit have the power to cure diseases. Prasad destroys sins and pains. To the faithless it brings very little benefit.Prasad is the sacred offerering of the Lord. The devotee offers sweet rice, fruits, milk and other such articles. After offering them to the Lord they are shared among the members of the household or the devotees present. The mental Bhav of the devotee offering the articles to the Lord is very important.

Do not neglect outward symbols. They are very beneficial. When viewed from the right angle of vision you will find that they play a very important part in your material as well as your spiritual life.

May you all tread the path of Dharma and attain Kaivalya Moksha (liberation) in this very birth.

AARATEE

JAYA JAYA AARATEE VIGHNAVINAAYAKA
VIGHNAVINAAYAKA SRI GANESHA

JAYA JAYA AARATI SUBRAHMANYA
SUBRAHMANYA KAARTIKEYA

JAYA JAYA AARATI VENUGOPAALA
VENUGOPAALA VENULOLA
PAAPAVIDURA NAVANEETA CHORA

JAYA JAYA AARATEE VENKATA RAMANA
VENKATA RAMANA SANKATA HARANA
SEETA RAAMA RADHE SHYAAMA

JAYA JAYA AARATEE GAURI MANOHARA
GAURI MANOHARA BHAVAANEE SHANKARA
SAMBA SADASIVA UMA MAHESHWARA

JAYA JAYA AARATEE RAAJA RAAJESHWAREE
RAAJA RAAJESHWAREE TRIPURA SUNDAREE
MAHAA LAKSHMEE MAHAA SARASWATEE
MAHAA KALI MAHAA SHAKTI

JAYA JAYA AARATEE AANJANEYA
AANJANEYA HANUMANTA
JAYA JAYA AARATEE DATTAATREYA
DATTAATREYA TRIMOORTI AVATAARA

JAYA JAYA AARATEE AADITYAYA
AADITYAYA BHAASKARAAYA
JAYA JAYA AARATEE SHANEESHWARAAYA
SHANEESHWARAAYA BHAASKARAAYA

JAYA JAYA AARTEE JESUS GURUDEV
MOSES GURDEV BUDHA GURUDEV
JAYA JAYA AARTEE MAHAVEERA
SHANKARACHARYA ADVITA GURU

JAYA JAYA AARATEE SADGURU NAATHA
SADGURU NAATHA SHIVAANANDA
JAYA JAYA AARATEE VISHNU DEVAANANDA
NADABRAHMANANDA
SAMASTA GURUBHYO NAMAHA

JAYA JAYA AARATEE VENU GOPAALA

TWAMEVA MATA

1. TWAMEVA MAATAA CHA PITAA TWAMEVA
   TWAMEVA BANDHUSCHA SAKHAA TWAMEVA
   TWAMEVA VIDYAA DRAVINAM TWAMEVA
   TWAMEVA SARVAM MAMA DEVA DEVA

2. KAAYENA VAACHAA MANASENDRIYARVAA
   BUDDHYAT MANAVAA PRAKRITIR SWABHAVAD
   KAROMI YAD YAD SAKALAM PARASMAI
   NARAYANAY ITI SAMARPAYAAMI

3. SARVADHARMAAN PARITYAJYA
   MAAMEKAM SHARANAM VRAJA
   AHAM TWAA SARVA PAAPEBHYO
   MOKSHA YISHYAA MIMAASHUCHA

MEANING

1 O God of Gods,
   Thou alone art my mother Thou art my father,
   Thou art my relatives my friend thou art
   Thou art my knowledge, Thuo art my learning
   Thou art my wealth, my all thou art.

2 Whatever actions I perform,
   whether by body, word, mind, senses, intellect, Atma,
   or the tendency of Nature,
   I dedicate all these to the Supreme Lord (Narayana).

3 Abandon all unrighteous deeds,
   Take refuge in Me alone.
   I will liberate you from all sins.
   Grieve not. (Bhagavad Gita.)

SHANTI MANTRAS

1. OM TRYAMBAKAM YAJAAMAHE
   SUGANDHIM PUSHTIVARDHANAM
   URVAARUKAMIVA BANDANAAN
   MRITYOR MUKSHEEYAMAAMRITAAT

2. OM SARVESHAAM SWASTIR BHAVATU
   SARVESHAAM SHANTIR BHAVATU
   SARVESHAAM POORNAM BHAVATU
   SARVESHAAM MANGALAM BHAVATU

3. SARVE BHAVANTU SUKHINAH
   SARVE SANTU NIRAAMAYAH
   SARVE BHADRAANI PASHYANTU
   MA KASCHID DUHKHA BHAAG BHAVET

4. OM ASATO MAA SAT GAMAYA
   TAMASO MAA JYOTIR GAMAYA
   MRITYOR MAA AMRITAM GAMAYA

5. OM POORNAMADAH POORNAMIDAM
   POORNAAT POORNAMUDACHYATE
   POORNASYA POORNAMAADAAYA
   POORNAMEVAAVASHISHYATE

   OM SHAANTIH SHAANTIH SHAANTIH

1. We worship the three-eyed One (Lord Siva),
   who is fragrant and who nourishes well all
   beings. May He liberate us from death for
   the sake of immortality even as the cucumber
   is severed from its bondage (to the creeper).

2. May auspiciousness be unto all
   May peace be unto all
   May fullness be unto all
   May prosperity be unto all

3. May all be happy
   May all be free from disabilities
   May all look to the good of others
   May none suffer from sorrow

4. Lead me from the unreal to the real
   From the darkness of ignorance to the light of knowledge
   From the fear of death to the abode of mortality.

5. That is whole, This is whole
   From that whole this whole becomes manifest
   From that whole when this whole is taken out
   What remains again is the whole
   Om Peace Peace Peace

O ADORABLE LORD OF MERCY AND LOVE
SALUTATIONS AND PROSTRATIONS UNTO THEE
THOU ART OMNIPRESENT, OMNIPOTENT AND OMNISCIENT
THOU ART SATCHIDANANDA
THOU ART EXISTENCE, KNOWLEDGE AND BLISS ABSOLUTE
THOU ART THE INDWELLER OF ALL BEINGS.
GRANT US AN UNDERSTANDING HEART, EQUAL VISION,
BALANCED MIND, FAITH, DEVOTION AND WISDOM.
GRANT US INNER SPIRITUAL STRENGTH
TO RESIST TEMPTATION AND TO CONTROL THE MIND.
FREE US FROM EGOISM, LUST, ANGER, GREED,
HATRED AND JEALOUSY.
FILL OUR HEARTS WITH DIVINE VIRTUES.
LET US BEHOLD THEE IN ALL THESE NAMES AND FORMS.
LET US SERVE THEE IN ALL THESE NAMES AND FORMS.
LET US EVER REMEMBER THEE.
LET US EVER SING THY GLORIES.
LET THY NAME BE EVER ON OUR LIPS.
LET US ABIDE IN THEE FOREVER AND EVER.

GAYATRI MANTRA

RAGA - Yaman Kalyan

> OM BHOOR BHUVAH SWAH TAT SAVITUR VARENYAM
> BHARGO DEVASYA DHEEMAHI DHIYO YO NAH PRACHO-
> DAYAAT

MEANING

> We meditate on that Ishwara's glory, Who has created the universe, Who
> is fit to be worshipped, Who is the embodiment of Knowledge and Light,
> Who is the remover of all sins and ignorance. May He enlighten our intellects.

DHYANA SHLOKAM

> SHANTAAKAARAM BHUJAGASHAYAHAM
> PADMANAABHAM SURESHAM
> VISHVADHAARAM GAGANSADRISAAM
> MEGHAVARNAM SHUBHAANGAM
> LAKSHMEEKAANTAM KAMALANAYANAM
> YOGIBHIRDHYAANAGAMYAM
> VANDE VISHNUM BHAVABHAYAHARAM
> SARVALOKAIKA NAATHAM

MEANING

> I bow to that Lord Vishnu, whose form is Peace, who is sleeping on the bed
> of snake (Adisesha), who has Lotus in the navel, who is Lord of gods, who
> is the support of this world, who is like ether, whose colour is like cloud,
> whose limbs are beautiful, who is the consort of the Goddess Lakshmi,
> whose eyes are like lotus, who is attainable by Yogins through meditation,
> who destroys the fear of Samsara, and who is the one Lord of all the worlds.

> KASTURI TILAKAM LALAATA PHALAKE
> VAKSHASTHALE KAUSTHUBHAM
> NASAGRE NAVA MAUKTIKAM JARA STHALE
> VENUM KARE KANKANAM
> SARVAANGE HARI CHANDANAM SULALITAM
> KANTHE CHA MUKTAAVALIM
> GOPASTREE PARIVESHTITO VIJAYATE
> GOPAALA ÇHOODAMANIH

MEANING

> On his forehead Kasturi is shining. On his chest a diamond is shining. On
> the front part of his nose nine pearls are shining. He is holding a flute in
> his hand.Chandan beautifies his whole body, his neck is shining with
> pearls. He is surrounded by the Gopis. He is like a most powerful jewel.

VANDANA HE SHAARADE

RAGA - Yaman Kalyan   TAL- Tintal

1. VANDANA HE SHAARADE
   TERE RAMYA MANOHAR MOORTI HRIDAY
   TERE MALA SOHAM SWASA RATAY
   TERE DARSHAN SE BHAVA TAAPA KATE
   VANDANA HE SHAARADE

2. KARAMEN PUSTAKA SPHATIKA MAALAA
   BINAAKE GUNJANA DIVYA RASAALA
   BHARE BHAKTI AURA JYNANA HAMOME
   TERE BAALAKA ME, TERE BAALAKA ME
   VANDANA HE SHAARADAE

3. JANMA DAIYEA MERE MAATAA
   PUNITA PREMA MAMATAA JAGATA
   PARAGHANA GHERA ANDHAYRAA MITAA DE
   JAGAAVE PARAMA PRAKAASHA
   MERE ANGA ME ANU ANU ME
   KEVALA TUMI HO MAATAA
   VANDANA HE SHAARADE

MEANING

1   I give salutations to you oh Lord.
    In my heart I always see your pure image.
    My every breath is repeating your name.
    With your darshan all the troubles of the world will go away.

2   I give salutations to you.
    In your hands you have a book and beads of pure stone.
    You create a divine atmosphere with your beautiful tunes.
    The sound of the Vina inspires us with devotion.
    We are your children.
    I give salutations to you.

3   You are our mother, you give me birth.
    I am filled with divine love and attachment to you.
    You put light in the deep darkness.
    You are creating supreme light.
    In all my limbs, with all my body,
    all the atoms in my heart,
    only you are (exist).I give salutations to you.

MAHAA LAKSHMEE   (Goddess of Wealth)

RAGA - Yaman   TAL - Tintal

1. OM MAHAA LAKSHMEE KAROTU KALYAANAM
   AAROGYA SUKHA SAMPRADA
   MAMASHATROU VINAASHAKE
   DEEPAJYOTI NAMASTUTE

2. OM SIDDHI BUDDHI PRADAADEVEE
   BHAKTI MUKTI PRADAYINEE
   MANTRA MOORTI SADAA DEVI
   MAHAA LAKSHMEE NAMASTUTE

3. OM NAMASTUTE MAHAA MAAYAA
   SHREE PEETAY SURPUJEETE
   SHANKH CHAKRA GADAA HASTE
   MAHAA LAKSHMEE NAMASTUTE

4. OM NAMASTUTE GURU VARE
   KULAA SUR BHAYANKARE
   SARVAPAAPA HARE DEVI
   MAHAA LAKSHMEE NAMASTUTE

5. OM SARVAJNYA SARVA DAY
   SARVA DUSHTABHAYAN KARE
   SARVA DUKH HARAY DEVI
   MAHAA LAKSHMEE NAMASTUTE

MEANING

1. O Mother Lakshmi please bless us. Provider of health and happiness. Destroyer of evil forces of mine. Please accept my salutations through lighted lamp.

2. O Provider of accomplishment and intelligence. Giver of devotion and salvation. You are the eternal image as Mantra. Salutations to that great Mother Lakshmi.

3. O I pray to thee, Maayaa, Creator of the Universe. I worship you provider of wealth, worshipped by the Gods. Your hands carry conch, chakra and gada. Salutations to that great Mother Lakshmi.

4. O I pray to thee teacher of teachers. Salutations to that great Mother Lakshmi.

5. O ever beautiful destroyer of enemies. Goddess who removes all unhappiness. Salutations to that great Mother Lakshmi.

DHANA LAKSHMEE

RAGA - Yaman   TAL - Tintal

DHANA LAKSHMEE DHANA DE TE ROHEE
SULA SULA BANA HAI

DHANA DHANA BAKO / NAYA NABE RAJA SAY
LAJA RA PEETA / SAWARI YA NAY
JA NAY ANTARA / DAY TAY ROHEE

DHANA LAKSHMEE DHANA P M G R G M P D N D P M G R S N S
DHANA LAKSHMEE DHANA S R G M P D N S S N D P M G R S N S
DHANA LAKSHMEE DHANA S N D N S R G R S N D P M G S N S

MEANING

O Mother Lakshmi, the giver of wealth and prosperity bless us so that we live in peace and happiness. Your blessings through wealth are visible in your eyes. You Beloved Lord are the protector of us all. You continue to provide for us without any reservation.

DEITY SHLOKAS

1. GAJAANANAM BHOOTA GANAADISEVITAM
   KAPITA JAMBUPHALA SAARA BHAKSHITAM
   UMAA SUTAM SHOKAVINASHAKAARANAM
   NAMAMI VIGHNESWARA PADA PANKAJAM

2. SHADAANANAM KUMKUMA RAKTAVARNAM
   MAHAA MATIM DIVYA MAYOORAVAAHANAM
   RUDRASYA SOONAM SURASAINYANAATHAM
   GUHAMSADAA HAM SHARANAM PRAPADYE

3. YAA KUNDENDU TUSHARAAHARA DHAVALA
   YAA SHUBHRA VASTRAAVRITAA
   YAA VEENA VARADANDA MANDITAKARAA
   YA ASWETA PADMAASANAA
   YAA BRAHMAACHYUTA SHANKARA PRABHRITIBHIR
   DEVAIH SADAA POOJITA
   SAA MAAM PAATU SARASVATEE BHAGAVATEE
   NISSHESHA JAADYAAPAHAA

4. OM NAMAH SHIVAYA GURAVE
   SATCHIDANANDA MOORTAYE
   NISHPRAPANCHAAYA SHANTAAYA
   SHRI SHIVAANANDAAYA TE NAMAH
   SHRI VISHNU DEVANANDAAYA TE NAMAH

5. SARVA MANGALA MAANGALYE
   SHIVE SARVAARTHASAADHIKE
   SHARANYE THRYAMBAKE GAURI
   NARAYANE NAMOSTUTE

MEANING

1   I prostrate myself before the lotus feet of Vigneshwara,
the son of Uma, the cause of destruction of sorrow,
who is served by the host of Bhuta-Ganas,
who has the face of an elephant,
who partakes of the essence of Kapittha and Jambu fruits.

2   I always take refuge in Guha of six faces,
who is of deep red color like kumkuma,
who is possessed of great knowledge,
who has the divine peacock to ride on,
who is the son of Rudra, and
who is the leader of the army of Gods.

3   May Goddess Saraswati, dispeller of all nescience and inertia,
whose complexion is like jasamine blossoms, moon or snow,
who is attired in spotless white Sari,
whose hands are adorned with enchanting Veena,
who is always worshipped by Brahma, Vishnu, Siva and other Gods,
who is seated in a white lotus, protect me.

4   Salutations to Guru Siva (Sivananda)
who is the embodiment of Existence - Knowledge - Bliss,
in whom worldliness does not exist, who is ever peaceful.
Salutations to Sri Sivananda and Sri Vishnu Devananda.

5   I salute the three-eyed Divine Mother Narayani,
who brings auspiciousness and
who fulfills all the desires of the Devotee (both spiritual and material).

SHANTI MANTRAS

1. OM SHAM NO MITRAH SHAM VARUNAHA
   SHAM NO BHAVATVARYAMAA
   SHAM NO INDRO BRIHASPATIH
   SHAM NO VISHNURURUKRAMAH
   NAMO BRAHMANE, NAMASTE VAAYO
   TWAMEVA PRATYAKSHAM BRAHMAASI
   TWAMEVA PRATYAKSHAM BHAMA VADISHYAAMI
   RITAM VADISHYAAMI, SATYAM VADISHYAAMI
   TANMAAMAVATU, TADVAKTAARAMAVATU
   AVATU MAAM AVATU VAKTAARAM
   OM SHAANTIH SHAANTIH SHAANTIH

2. OM SAHANAAVAVATU,
   SAHANAU BHUNAKTU
   SAHA VEERYAM KARAVAAVAHAI
   TEJASVI NAAVADHEETAMASTU
   MAA VIDVISHAAVAHAI
   OM SHAANTIH SHAANTIH SHAANTIH

3. OM AAPYAYANTU MAMANGAANI
   VAAK PRAANASCHAKSHUH SHROTRAMATHO
   BALAMINDRIYAANI CHA SARVAANI
   SARVAM BRAHMOPANISHADAM
   MAAHAM BRAHMA NIRAKURYAAM
   MAA MAA BRAHMA NIRAAKAROT
   ANIRAKARANAMASTU
   ANIRAKARANAM ME ASTU
   TADAATMANI NIRATE
   YA UPANISHATSU DHARMAH
   TE MAYI SANTU TE MAYI SANTU
   OM SHAANTIH SHAANTIH SHAANTIH

4. OM BHADRAM KARNEBHIH SHRINUYAAMA DEVAAH
   BHADRAM PASHYEMAAKSHABHIRYAJATRAAH
   STHIRAIRANGAISTUSHTUVAAMSASTANOOBHIR
   VYASHEMAHI DEVAHITAM YADAAYUH
   SWASTI NA INDRO VRIDDHASHRAVAAH
   SWASTI NAH POOSHA VISHVAVEDAAH
   SWASTI NAS TAARKSHYO ARISHTANEMIH
   SWASTI NO BRIHASPATIRDADHAATU
   OM SHAANTI SHAANTISHAANTI

MEANING

1   May Mitra, Varuna and Aryama be good to us.
May Indra and Brihaspati and
Vishnu of great strides be good to us.
Prostrations to the Brahman. Prostrations to Thee.
O Vayu Thou art the visible Brahman.
I shall proclaim Thee as visible Brahman.
I shall call Thee the Just and the True.
May He protect the teacher and me.
May He protect the teacher. Om Peace, Peace, Peace.

2   Om, May He protect us both (teacher and taught)
May He cause us both to enjoy the bliss of liberation.
May we both exist to find out the true meaning of the scriptures.
May our studies be fruitful.
May we never quarrel with each other.
Let there be threefold Peace.

3   May my limbs, speech, Prana, eye, ear and
vital energy of all my senses grow vigorous.
All is the Brahman of the Upanishads.
May I never deny the Brahman.
May the Brahman never desert me.
Let that relationship endure.
Let the virtues recited in the Upanishads be rooted in me.
May they repose in me.
Om Peace, Peace, Peace.

4   Om O Worshipful ones,
may our ears hear what is auspicious.
May we see what is auspicious.
May we sing your praise,
live our alloted span of life in perfect health and strength.
May Indra extolled in the scriptures,
Pushan the all knowing Tarkshya who saves from all harm, and
Brihaspati who protects our spiritual lustre,
vouchsafe prosperity in our study of the scriptures and
the practise of the truths contained therein.
Om Peace, Peace, Peace.

HYMNS TO THE GURU

1. BRAHMAANANDAM PARAMASUKHADAM
   KEVALAM JNANAMOORTIM
   DVANDVAATEETAM GAGANA SADRISHAM
   TATVAMASYAADI LAKSHYAM
   EKAM NITYAM VIMALAM ACHALAM
   SARVADHEE SAAKSHIBHOOTAM
   BHAAVAATEETAM TRIGUNA RAHITAM
   SAT GURUM TAM NAMAAMI

2. CHAITANYAM SHAASWATAM SHAANTAM
   NIRAAKAARAM NIRANJANAM
   NAADA BINDU KAALAATEETAM
   TASMAI SREE GURAVE NAMAH

3. GURUR BRAHMAA GURUR VISHNU
   GURUR DEVO MAHESHWARAH
   GURU SAAKSHAAT PARAMBRAHMA
   TASMAI SREE GURAVE NAMAH

4. AJNAANA TIMIRAANDHASYA
   JNAANAANJANA SHALAAHKAYAA
   CHAKSHUR UNMEELITAM YENA
   TASMAI SREE GURAVE NAMAH

5. DHYAANA MOOLAM GUROR MOORTIH
   POOJA MOOLAM GUROH PADAM
   MANTRA MOOLAM GUROR VAAKYAM
   MOKSHA MOOLAM GUROH KRIPAA

6. OM NAMAHSHIVAAYA GURAVE
   SATCHIDANANDA MOORTAYE
   NISHPRAPANCHAAYA SHAANTAAYA
   SREE SIVANANDAAYA TE NAMAH
   OM SREE VISHNUDEVANANDAAYA TE NAMAH

MEANING

1   I salute the Guru who is the incarnation of supreme bliss, who is the bestower of bliss, who is independent, who is the embodiment of the highest wisdom, who is beyond the pairs of opposites, who is all pervading like space, who is the goal pointed out by sacred formulae like "That Thou Art", who is one without a second, who is eternal, pure and unmoving, who is the witness of all hearts, who is beyond our imagination and who is free from the play of the qualities of Nature.

2   Salutations to the Guru who is awareness itself, eternal, peaceful, formless and free from blemish, who is beyond Nada, Bindu and Kala.

3   Guru is the Creator (of our spiritual aspirations), the Protector (of our aspirations) and the Great Lord (who destroys the evil in us); and the Guru himself is the Supreme Being. Salutations to the Guru.

4   Salutations to the Guru who by the collyrium of Wisdom removes the-blinding darkness of ignorance and opens the inner eye that perceives the Truth.

5   The Guru's form (or image) is fit to be meditated upon; the feet of the Guru should be worshipped; the Guru's words should be regarded as Mantra or Gospel Truth; and the Guru's Grace will bestow liberation on us.

6   Salutations to Guru Siva, who is the embodiment of Existence-Knowledge -Bliss Absolute, in whom worldliness does not exist, who is ever peaceful. Salutations to Sivananda. Salutations to Vishnu Devananda.

UNIVERSAL PRAYER OF SWAMI SIVANANDA

O ADORABLE LORD OF MERCY AND LOVE
SALUTATIONS AND PROSTRATIONS UNTO THEE
THOU ART OMNIPRESENT, OMNIPOTENT AND OMNISCIENT
THOU ART SATCHIDANANDA
THOU ART EXISTENCE, KNOWLEDGE AND BLISS ABSOLUTE
THOU ART THE INDWELLER OF ALL BEINGS.
GRANT US AN UNDERSTANDING HEART, EQUAL VISION,
BALANCED MIND, FAITH, DEVOTION AND WISDOM.
GRANT US INNER SPIRITUAL STRENGTH
TO RESIST TEMPTATIONS AND TO CONTROL THE MIND.
FREE US FROM EGOISM, LUST, ANGER, GREED,
HATRED AND JEALOUSY.
FILL OUR HEARTS WITH DIVINE VIRTUES.
LET US BEHOLD THEE IN ALL THESE NAMES AND FORMS.
LET US SERVE THEE IN ALL THESE NAMES AND FORMS.
LET US EVER REMEMBER THEE.
LET US EVER SING THY GLORIES.
LET THY NAME BE EVER ON OUR LIPS.
LET US ABIDE IN THEE FOREVER AND EVER

1 HARI NAARAAYANA GOVINDA
   JAYA JAGAT NAARAAYANA GOVINDA
   NAARAAYANA NAARAAYANA NAARAAYANA OM

   Hari, Narayana and Govinda
   are the ruler and preservor of the Universe.

2. RAAMACHANDRA RAGHUVEERA
   RAAMCHANDRA RANADHEERA
   RAAMACHANDRA RAGHUNAATHA
   RAAMACHANDRA JAGANNAATHA
   RAAMACHANDRA MAMA BANDHU
   RAAMACHANDRA JAYA SINDHU

   Ramachandra, Hero of the Raghu Race
   Ramachandra Radiant on the battlefield
   Ramachandra Lord of Raghus
   Ramachandra Lord of the Universe
   Ramachandra My Brother
   Ramachandra The ocean of mercy

3 BOLE NAATHA UMAPATE
   SHAMBHU SHANKARA PASHUPATE
   NANDI VAAHANA NAAGA BHOOSHANA
   CHANDRA SHEKARA JATAA DHAARAA
   GIRIJAA RAMANA SADAASHIVA

   The simple hearted Lord (consort of Uma -
   the energy aspect of the Universe),
   Shambu the Lord of the animal kingdom.
   Who rides on the bull and who decorates
   himself with snakes.
   The crescent moon decorates his crown.
   Siva, who is accompanying Uma.

4 NARAAYANA NARAAYANA JAYA GOVINDA HARE
   NARAAYANA NARAAYANA JAYA GOPALA HARE

   Names of Lord Vishnu
   The Divine aspect of Preservation
   Glory to Lord Narayana

5   GOVINDA JAYA JAYA
    GOPAALA JAYA JAYA
    RAADHAARAMANA HARI
    GOVINDA JAYA JAYA

    Victory to Govinda (Krishna)
    Victory to Gopala (Krishna)
    Consort of Radha, Hari, Govinda
    Glory Glory

6   NATARAAJ NATARAAJA
    SIVAANANDA NATARAJA
    SIVARAAJ SIVARAAJA
    SIVAANANDA SIVARAAJA

    Siva, the great ruler of the Universe
    Siva, the God of Cosmic Dance

7   HARI HARI BOL, BOL HARI BOL
    MUKUNDA MADHAVA GOVINDA BOL
    HARI BOL HARI BOL

    Sing the glories of the Lord
    Chant Krishna's names.

8   BANSUREE BANSUREE BANSUREE SHYAAMAKEE
    HE RAAMA
    HE KRISHNA
    HE BUDDHA
    HE JESUS
    HE ALLAH
    HARI BOL, SHIVA BOL
    I AM THINE ALL IS THINE
    OH MY LORD ALL IS THINE
    BANSUREE BANSUREE BANSUREE SHYMAKEE

    Bansuri is the name of the bamboo flute that Lord Krishna plays.It repre-
    sents the individual soul that is empty of the gross ego, thus making it pos-
    sible for the Lord to play his divine tune through him.He becomes that per-
    fect instrument through whom Divine Inspiration flows

1. HARE RAAMA HARE RAAMA RAAMA RAAMA HARE HARE
    HARE KRISHNA HARE KRISHNA KRISHNA KRISHNA HARE HARE

    RAGHU PATI RAAGHAVA RAAJAA RAAM
    PATITA PAAVANA SEETAA RAAM

    HARE RAAMA HARE RAAMA RAAMA RAAMA HARE HARE
    HARE KRISHNA HARE KRISHNA KRISHNA KRISHNA HARE HARE

    HARI HARI BOL BOL HARI BOL
    MUKUNDA MADHAVA GOVINDA BOL

2. SHREE RAAM JAYA RAAM JAYA JAYA RAAM OM
    SHREE RAAM JAYA RAAM JAYA JAYA RAAM

    JAYA SEETAA RAAM JAYA JAYA HANUMAAN
    SAT GURU DEVAANANDA BHAGAVAAN
    SAT GURU DEV SIVAANANDA BHAGAVAAN

3. JAI SEETAA RAAM JAI SEETAA RAAM
    JAYA HANUMAAN HARI HARI BOL

4. RAGHU PATI RAGHAVA RAJA RAAM
    PATITA PAAVANA SEETAA RAAM

    SEETAA RAAM SEETAA RAAM SEETAA RAAM
    JAYA RADHESHYAAM
    RADHESHYAAM RADHESHYAAM RADHESHYAAM
    JAYA RADHESHYAAM

    ISHWARA ALLAAH TERE NAM
    SABAKO SANMATI DE BHAGAVAAN
    THE PATHS ARE MANY BUT THE TRUTH IS ONE
    LOVE THY NEIGHBOR AS THYSELF
    MOSES, BUDDHA IS THY NAME
    LOVE THY NEIGHBOR AS THYSELF

    ALLAH, KRISHNA IS THY NAME
    LOVE THY NEIGHBOR AS THYSELF
    KRISHNA, RAMA IS THY NAME
    LOVE THY NEIGHBOR AS THYSELF

    RAGHUPATHI RAAGHAVA RAAJAA RAAM
    PATITHA PAAVANA SEETAA RAAM

Ram is He who is born in the Raghu Clan,
Lord Ram, Purifier of Sinners and Beloved of Sita.
Glory be to the Beloved of Radha (who is Shyam or Krishna).
Beloved of Radha,
Victory to Shyama (Glory).
Ishwara and Allah are Thy Names
Give to all wisdom so that we may transend petty differences.

5. AYODHYAA VAASI RAAM RAAM
   DASHARATHA NANDANA RAAM RAAM
   PATITA PAAVANA JANAKEE JEEVANA
   SEETA MOHANA RAAM

6. EHI MUDAM DEHI ME SREE KRISHNA KRISHNA
   PAAHI MAM GOPAALA BAALA KRISHNA KRISHNA

   NANDAA GOPA NANDANA SREE KRISHNA KRISHNA
   VRINDAAVANA CHANDRA SREE KRISHNA KRISHNA

   RAADHAA MANO MOHANA SREE KRISHNA KRISHNA
   MADHAVA DAYANIDHE SREE KRISHNA KRISHNA

   BHAKTA PARIPAALANA SREE KRISHNA KRISHNA
   BHAKTI MUKTI DAAYAKA SREE KRISHNA KRISHNA

   GOPEEJANA VALLABHA SREE KRISHNA KRISHNA
   GOPA KULA PAALAKA SREE KRISHNA KRISHNA

   SARVA LOKA NAAYAKA SREE KRISHNA KRISHNA
   SARVA JAGAN MOHANA SREE KRISHNA KRISHNA

   Give me this Bliss, O Krishna, O cowherd boy. I take refuge in Thee.

   O Krishna, delight of Nanda and Gopas,the Moon of Brindavan.

   O Krishna, enchanter of the mind of Radha.
   O Madhava (consort of Maha Lakshmi), Ocean of Compassion.

   Protector of devotees. Bestower of devotion and liberation.
   The beloved of the Gopis, Protector of the Gopas.
   The Leader of the whole world, Enchanter of the entire universe.

7. SHAILA GIREESHWARA UMAA MAHESWARA
   KAASHI VISHWESHWAR SADAASIVA
   SADAASIVA SADAASIVA
   SADAASIVA SHAMBO SADAASIVA

8. GOURI SUTAYA OM NAMAH OM
   LAMBODARAAYA OM NAMAH OM
   VIGHNESHWARAAYA OM NAMA OM
   OM NAMAH OM
   BHAVADUKHA BHANJANA OM NAMA OM

9. MURALI KRISHNA MUKUNDA KRISHNA
   MOHANA KRISHNA KRISHNA KRISHNA

   GOPI KRISHNA GOPAALA KRISHNA
   GOVARDHANADHAARA KRISHNA KRISHNA

   RAADHAA KRISHNA BAALA KRISHNA
   RASA VILOLA KRISHNA KRISHNA

   GOKULA KRISHNA YASHODAA KRISHNA
   DEVAKEE NANDANA KRISHNA KRISHNA

10. SHIVA SHIVA MAHAADEVA NAMA SHIVAAYA SADAASHIVA
    SHIVA SHIVA MAHAADEVA NAMAH SHIVAYA SADAASHIVA
    HARE RAAMA HARE RAAMA RAAMA RAAMA HARE HARE
    HARE KRISHNA HARE KRISHNA KRISHNA KRISHNA HARE HARE

    NARAAYANA HARI NARAAYANA HARI NARAAYANA HARI
    OM(2X)

    BHAGAVAAN SREE SIVAANANDA BHAGAVAAN SREE
       SIVAANANDA OM(2X)
    GURU MAHAARAAJ GURU DEVO (3X) SAT GURU SIVAANANDA

    OM HARI OM HARI OM HARI OM HARI OM HARI OM HARI
    OM(2X)
    OM RAAMA.......
    OM KRISHNA.......
    OM BUDDHA........
    OM MAHAAVEERA.......
    OM MOSES.........
    OM JESUS.......
    OM ALLAH......
    OM DEVEE.......
    OM SHAKTI......
    OM AIM HREEM KLEEM.........

    SHIVA SHIVA MAHAADEVA NAMAH SHIVAYA SADAA SHIVA
    SHIVA SHIVA MAHAADEVA NAMAH SHIVAYA SADAA SHIVA

11. SHAMBHO MAHAADEVA CHANDRA CHOODA
    SHANKARA SAAMBA SADAASIVA
    GANGADHARA HARA KAILAASA VAASA
    PAHIMAAM PARVATIRAMANA
    SIVAAYA SIVAAYA SIVAAYA NAMAHOM
    HARAAYA HARAAYA HARAAYA NAMAHOM
    NAMAH SIVAAYA NAMAH SIVAAYA

12. JAI SIVA SHANKARA BHUM BHUM HARA HARA
    HARA HARA HARA HARA HARA BOL HARA
    SIVA SIVA SIVA SIVA SIVA AADI SUNDARA
    HARA HARA HARA HARA HARA AADI SUNDARA
    HEY PARAMESHWARA DAYA KARO

13. SAAMBA SADAASHIVA SAAMBA SADAASHIVA
    SAAMBA SADAASHIVA SAAMBA SHIVOM HARA

    OM MAATAA OM MAATAA OM SREE MAATAA JAGAD MAATAA
    OM MAATAA OM MAATAA OM SREE MAATAA JAGADAMBA

    UMA PARAMESWAREE SREE BHUVANESWAREE
    ADI PARA SHAKTI DEVEE MAHESHWAREE

14. OM BHAGAVAAN
    SREE BHAGAVAAN
    AANANDA BHAGAVAAN
    SIVAANANDA BHAGAVAAN

15. JAYA OM MAATAA JAYA JAGADAMBA
    RAAJA RAAJESHWARI
    SREE PARAATPAREE

16. HARA HARA MAHAADEVA SHAMBO
    KAASHI VISWANAATHA GANGE.

BHAJAN 1

NAMO BHUTANAATHA

RAGA - Darbari Kanada   TAL- Keherwa

1. NAMO BHUTANAATHA, NAMO PARVATEESHA
   NARA RUNDHA MAALAA DHAARI
   VISHA SARPA TE SHAREERE
   DAMARU TRISHOOLA VAALAA
   KONI BHETAVE AMALA; NAMO.........

2. VYAAGHRA SANE VIRAJE
   LALAATA CHANDRA SAJE
   AVADHOOTA VESHA WAALAA
   KONI BHETAVE AMALA; NAMO......

3. SHOBHE JATETE GANGAA
   PIVO NIRAYI BHANGAA
   ALAMASTA BAILA WAALAA
   KONI BHETAVE AMALA; NAMO....

4. NACHE PISHYACHI SANGE
   JOBHI LINI SARANGE
   VAASA HOVE BHAWI KALA
   KONI BHETAVE AMALA; NAMO....

5. KARI SHANKHA NAADA RUNJE
   MUKHE RAMA NAMA GUNJE
   KSHANI JALI LE MADALA
   KONI BHETAVE AMALA; NAMO....

MEANING

1   Prostrations to the Lord of the Bhootas ,Lord of Parvati.He who wears the garland of skulls and poisonous snakes on his body.He holds the Damaru, the rhythm of creation and the Trishul, the symbol of the three gunas, the forces of creation.

2   Seated on a tiger,master of the senses,the moon shining on your forehead.Who wears nothing but ash, symbol of complete renunciation. No one is better than you.

3   Ganga brings glory from the matted locks.He who drank the intoxicating drink and is always seated on his strong bull.

4   He dances in the company of spirits, becoming just like them.

5   He blows the conch, symbolizing the Nadam of creation.
    He sings Rama's name. He takes away all problems.

SUMIRANA KARA LE

RAGA - Yaman Kalyan   TAL - Keherwa

> SUMIRANA KARA LE MERE MANAA RE
> TERI BEETA GAYI UMARA HARI NAAMA BINAA RE
> SUMIRANA KARA LE

1. KOOPA NIRA BINU DHENU KSHEERA BINU
   DHARATI MEHA BINAA
   JAISE TARUWARA PHALA BINA HINAA
   TAISE PRAANI HARI NAMA BINA RE
   SUMIRANA KARA LE

2. DEHA NAINA BINA RAINA CHANDRA BINA
   MANDIRA DEEPA BINAA
   JAISE PANDITA VEDA VIHINAA
   TAISE PRAANI HARI NAAMA BINAA RE
   SUMIRANA KARA LE

3. KAAMA KRODHA MADA LOBHA NIHAARO
   CHHANDA DE ABA SANTA JANA
   KAHE NANAKA SAHA SUNO BHAGAWANTAA
   YA JAGA ME NAHI KOI APANAA RE
   SUMIRANA KARA LE

MEANING

Oh my friend, now, remember God and chant his Name.
Your life is passing away without uttering his name.

1   As a well without water, a cow without milk,
    earth without rain, as a tree without fruits,
    So is life without Hari's name.

2   As a body without eyes, a sky without moon,
    a temple without light, as a Pandit without Vedas,
    So is life without Hari's name.

3   Oh good man, give up desire, anger, pride and greed .
    Seek the company of Saints and Sages.
    Says Guru Nanak, listen brothers,
    while you are here in this world, no one is for you,
    always sing and chant Hari's Name

CHALO MANA

RAGA - Yaman Kalyan   TAL - Keherwa

> CHALO MANA GANGAA JAMUNAA TIRA

1. CHALO MANA
    GANGAA JAMUNAA
    NIRAMALA PAANI
    SHEETAL HOTA SHAREERA
    CHALO MANA GANGAA JAMUNAA TIRA

2. MORA MUKUTA PE
    TAAMBARA SHOBHE
    KUNDALA JALAKATA HEERA
    CHALO MANA GANGAA JAMUNAA TIRA

3. BANSI BAJAAWATA
    GAAWATA KANHA
    SANGA LIYA BALABEER
    CHALO MANA GANGAA JAMUNAA TIRA

4. MEERA KAHAI PRABHO
    GIRIDHARA NAAGARA
    CHARANAKAMALA PARA SHIRA
    CHALO MANA GANGAA JAMUNAA TIRA

MEANING

1   O Mind, let's go to the banks of the Ganga and Yamuna where
    their cold water will make our body cool.
    O Mind, let's go to the banks of the Ganga and Yamuna.

2   A yellow robe adorns him and
    a crown of peacock feathers is shining.

3   Krishna is there playing the flute and singing.
    With him is Balaram (Krishna's brother).

4   Meera says: O Krishna I bow my head down to
    the lotus flower feet of yours.

NAARAAYANA KAA NAAMA NIRAALA

RAGA - Desh   TAL - Keherwa

1. NAARAAYANA KAA NAAMA NIRAALAA
   USAKI MAHIMAA NYAARI RE
   USAKI MAHIMAA NYAARI RE
   USAKI LILAA NYAARI RE; NAARAAYANA...

2. MACHHA KACHHA KE ROOPA MEN AAYAA
   ROOPA VARAAHAKA DHAARAA
   WAMANA BANA NAARAAYANA ME
   USA BALIVIRA KO MAARAA
   NARASIMHA BANA KE HIRANAA KASHA KE
   NAAVA JAGATA SE NYAARI RE; NAARAAYANA...

3. NARA NAARAAYANA EKA HAI DONO
   YAHA SAMAJHA MEN AAYE
   NARA NAARAAYANA BANA SAKATA HAI
   SATYA KE JO APANAAYE
   JAY NAARAAYANA JAY JAY
   BHAKTANA KE HITAKAARI RE; NAARAAYANA...

MEANING

1   There is nothing to compare the greatness of Narayan's name with.
    His glories and Leelas (world play) are unfathomable.

2   He first came in the form of a fish, and
    then a tortoise and then a boar.
    He took the form of Varaha (a dwarf).
    Also Narayana became Vamana and he killed that brave Bali.
    In Narasimha's form he killed Hiranya Kashyapu and
    liberated his soul from these nine worlds.
    Whenever the balance of creation is threatened
    Lord Narayana incarnates in whatever form is necessary
    to restore the balance and preserve the creation.

3. Understand this truth that Man and God, both are One.
    Realize this truth and be free.
    Victory to the Great Lord Narayana.

RAAMA RATAN DHAN PAYO

RAGA - Pilu   TAL - Keherwa

PAYO JI MAINAY / RAM RATAN DHAN PAYO

1. VASTU AMOLAK DI MERE SATGURU
   KIRPA KAR APANAAYO
   PAYO....

2. JANMA JANMAKEE POONJI PAYI
   JAGME SABHI KHOVAYO
   PAYO....

3. KHARACHAI NAHI KOYI CHOR NA LOOTAY
   DIN DIN BARHAT SAVAAYO
   PAYO.....

4. SATKI NAAV KHEVATIYA SATGURU
   BHAVA SAGAR TARA AAYO
   PAYO.....

5. MIRAAKE PRABHU GIRIDHAR NAAGAR
   HARAKH HARAKH JAS GAAYO
   PAYO.....

MEANING

1. I verily have gotten the greatest wealth,
   the jewel that is Rama's Name.
   This most invaluable wealth was given to me by my preceptor.
   With mercy, he made me his own.

2. This treasure is attained after many incarnations.
   This gives me dispassion for the world.

3. This treasure does not diminish by using it.
   Thieves can't steal it.
   Day by day it increases more and more.

4. Using the boat of truth and the Guru as the navigator,
   the ocean of worldliness can be crossed.

5. Mira's Lord is the clever Krishna
   Who lifted the mountain of Govardhana with one hand.
   She happily sings His glory.

NAARAAYANA KO BHAJAN KARO

RAGA - Bheempalas   TAL - Keherwa

> NAARAAYANA KO BHAJANA KARO NARA
> MUKTI NA HO BINAA BHAJANA TUMHAREE
> NAARAAYANA KO BHAJANA KARO NARA

1. KYA KASHI JAVE
   KYA MATHURA JAVE
   KYA KAASHI JAVE P M P G M PN D P M P G M P M P
   KYA KAASHI JAVE
   KYA MATHURA JAVE
   KYA KEDAAR JAVE
   KYA BADAREE JAVE
   KYA PARAVATA BANA PHIRATA ANAREE
   MUKTI NA HO BINAA BHAJANA TUMHAREE

2. JAPA TAPA YOGA KATHINA KALI MAYI
   SHASTRA ANEKA PADO DINA RATI / MUKTI NA......

3. BHAI BANDHU AURA KUTUMBA PARUWAARA
   KISAKI HO TUMA KAUNA TIHAARA
   SABA APA APANA MATALABA WALA
   KAHATA KABIR SUNNO BHAI SADHO
   AAPA GAYE PICHE DOOBAGAYI DUNIYA / MUKTI NA....

MEANING

Oh man do bhajans of Narayana
Without bhajans of God liberation is not obtained.

1   Why are you wandering in vain and to all the places of pilgrimage (Kashi, Mathura, Kedar, Badrinath).This will not give you liberation. Only by singing the name of god will you get Mukti.

2   All these other paths Japa, Austerity and Yoga are very difficult. You may read the scriptures day and night but Mukti will not come without Bhajans of Narayana.

3   Brothers, sisters, relatives and family members, to whom do you belong and who belongs to you. Everyone is selfish and looks to their own welfare. Kabir says, Listen good man, when you are dead and gone, the whole world is gone.

LAGAA LE PREMA ISHWARA SE

RAGA - Bhairavi Tal - Keherwa

LAGAA LE PREMA ISHWARA SE
AGAR TOO MOOKSHA CHAHATA HAI

NAHEE VO PAATAAL KE ANDAR
NAHEE VO AKAASH KE UPAR

SADAA VO PAAS HAI TE RE
KAHAAN DHUNDHATA JAATAA HAI

MEANING

If you wish for liberation
give all the love of your heart to the Lord.

He is not somewhere hidden under the earth.
Nor is he somewhere above the sky.

He is always with you.
He is closer to you than anything you can think of.
Where are you going about searching for Him?

YAMUNA TEERA VIHAARI

RAGA - Yaman   TAL - Keherwa

YAMUNA TEERA VIHAARI
VRINDAAVAN SANCHAAREE
GOVARDHAN GIRI DHAAREE
GOPALA KRISHNA MURAARI

1. DASHARATHA NANDANA RAAM RAAM
   DASHA MUKHA MARDANA RAAM RAAM
   PASHUPATI RANJANA RAAM RAAM
   PAAPA VIMOCHANA RAAM RAAM

2. MANIMAYA BHOOSHANA RAAM RAAM
   MANJULA BHAASHANA RAAM RAAM
   RENEJAYA BHEESHANA RAAM RAAM
   RAGHUKULA BHOOSHANA RAAM RAAM

MEANING

Who sports at the banks of Yamuna;
Who moves in Brindavan;
Who lifted Govardhana Mountain,
He is Gopala (Protector ofCows), KrishnaMurari (Destroyer of demon Mura).

1   Ram is the son of Dasaratha.
     Ram is the destroyer of ten headed Ravana.
     Ram is the delight of Lord Siva.
     Ram is the dispeller of all sins.

2   Glory to Sri Radha
     Glory to the son of Nanda (Krishna).
     Glory,
     Glory to the delighter of the minds of Gopis.

KAISE KAISE JAHUN

RAGA - Pilu   TAL - Keherwa

KAISE KAISE JAHUN
PANIYA BHARANA

HE NANDA LALA
ROKE MERI VAATA
KAISE KAISE JAHUN.......

MAI JAMUNAA JALA BHARANA JATITI
CHUNARI PAKARA MANA LINAA CHINA DI

MEANING

How will I go? O Son of Nanda (Krishna)
You are hindering my path.

How will I go to the Jamuna River to fetch water?
You are Holding my sari,
and making mischief with me,
you have stolen away my heart.

BHAJAN 2

SHRI RAAMACHANDRA

RAGA - Bhairav   TAL - Rupak

SHRI RAAMACHANDRA KRIPAALU BHAJAMANA
HARANA BHAVABHAYADAARUNAM
NAVA KANJA LOCHANA KANJA MUKHAKARA
KANJA PADAKANJAARANAM

1. KANDARPA AGANITA AMITA CHABI NAVA
   NEELA NEERAJA SUNDARAM
   PATA PEETA MAANAHU THADITA RUCHI SHUCHI
   NUMI JANAKA SUTAAVARAM

2. BHAAJA DEENABANDHU DINESHA DANAVA
   DAITYA VANSHA NIKANDANAM
   RAGHU NANDA AANANDA KANDA KAUSHALA
   CHANDA DASHARATHA NANDANAM

3. SHIRA MUKUTA KUNDALA TILAKA CHAARU
   UDAARA ANGA VIBHOOSHANAM
   AAJAANU BHUJA SHARA CHAAPADHARA SANGRAAM
   JITA KHARA DUSHANAM

4. ITI VADATHI TULASIDAASA SHANKARA
   SHESHA MUNI MANA RANJANAM
   MAMA HRIDAYA KUNJA NIVASA KARU KAAMADI
   KHALADALA GANJANAM

SHRI RAAMACHANDRA KRIPALU BHAJAMANA
HARANA BHAVA BHAYA DARUNAM
NAVA KANJA LOCHANA KANJA MUKHA KARA
KANJA PADA KANJAARANAM

MEANING

Let my mind worship merciful Shri Rama
who removes unbearable fears from the world.
His eyes, face and feet are like newly opened red lotus flower.

1   His infinite everlasting image is as beautiful as
      the shadows of blue lotus in the water which looks like
      countless mirrors collected together and creates a glow.
      The husband of Janaka's daughter is a savior of people in distress.

2   I worship Shri Ram who is friend of the poor and
      who is the destroyer of evils and devils.
      Descendant of Raghu dynasty and son of Dasharat,
      Shri Ram is the embodiment of eternal joy.

3   Crown on his head and plenty of jewels and pearls on his body
      makes him more and more beautiful.
      His strong mighty arms carries bow and arrows
      with which he wins Kara and Dushanama (evil forces) in the war.

4   Tulsidas says: Shri Ram who provides happiness and
      joy to Lord Shiva and other saints,
      also rests in the depth of my heart and
      destroys desires, temptations and evil thoughts.

PRABHO DATTAA RE

RAGA - Bhairav   TAL - Tintal

   1. PRABHO DATTAA RE
       NA KARE MAN JEEVAN GHARI PHALA CHINA
       PRABHO DATTAA RE

   2. JO TU CHAHE ANA DHANA LAKSHMI
       DOODHA POOTA BAHOO TERE
       WA KO NAAMA BHAJA GURU KA NAAM
       PRABHO DATTAA RE

MEANING

1   Datta Lord is the Giver.
      Don't be proud of life for an hour, a minute, a second.
      God is the Giver.

2   You desire a lot of food, wealth, prosperity and
      offspring, But remember Guru's name.

MERE TO GIRIDHAR GOPAALA

RAGA - Gurjar Todi   TAL - Dadra

1. MERE TO GIRIDHAR GOPAALA
   DOOSARAA NA KOYEE

2. JAA KE SHIRA MORA MUKUTA
   MERO PATI SOYEE
   SHANKHA CHAKRA GADAA PADMA
   KANTHE MAALAA SOYEE

3. CHANDI DAYEE KULKI KAHA NEE
   KA KARI HAI KOYEE
   SANTANA DIGA BAITHI BAITHI
   LOKA LAJA KHOYEE

4. AASU WANA JALA SINCHI SINCHI
   PREMA BAILEE BOYEE
   ABA TO BAAT PHAILEE GAYEE
   JANAY SABA KOYEE

5. BHAGATE DEKHEE RA JEE HUEE
   JAGATEE DAYKHEE ROYEE
   DAASEE MEERA LAALAA GIRIDHARA
   TAA RO AAB MOHEE

MEANING

1   My beloved is that Giridhar Gopal.
    There is no other.

2   On whose head there is a crown of peacock feathers.
    In his hands there is Sanka, Chakra, Gadaa and Lotus.
    On his neck is a mala. Such a one is my husband.

3   I have renounced the relation of any family.
    In this world who can do anything to me.
    Sitting in the company of saints I have no shame

4   The tears of my eyes are flowing.
    The creeper of devotion of love I have planted has sprouted.
    Everyone knows that I belong to God.

5   Wherever I see the devotee of God I feel very happy,
    but whenever I see people engrossed in worldly affairs I feel sad.
    Giridhar is my master and I his servant. Please rescue me Lord.

SHANKARA TERE

RAGA - Shivaranjani   TAL - Jaleka

.   SHANKAR TERE JATAA MEN BAHATEE HAI GANGA DHARA
KAALI GHATAA KE ANDARA JIMIDAA MINI UJAARAA

1.   GALE MUNDA MAALAA SAJE
SASI BAALA ME BIRAAJE
DAMARU NE NAADA BAAJE
KARA MEN TRISULA DHAARAA

2.   DRIGA TEENA TEJA RASI
KATI BANDA NAAGA PHASI
GIRIJAH SANGA DASI
SABA VISHWA KE AADHAARAA

3.   MRIGA CHARMA VASANA DHARI
BRISA RAJA PAISA VAARI
NIJA BHAKTA DUKHAHAARI
KAILASA ME BIHAARAA

4.   SHIVA NAAM JO UCHAARE
SAB PAAP DOSA TARE
BRAHMAA NANDA NABHI SARE
BHAVASINDHU PARATAARE

MEANING

Oh Lord Siva the river Ganga flows from your matted locks.
It shines like a lightening in black clouds.

1   On his neck is a garland of skull, a
crescent moon is on his head. His drums
make a loud sound.In his hand is the trident.

2   His three eyes are full of light.
The serpent is wound on his hand. He
is Uma or Parvati's servant, Supporter
of the whole universe.

3   He who wears the deer skin rides on a bull.
Destroyer of the suffering of his true devotees.
He who is seated in Kailasa .

4   He who sings the name of Siva will have all sins destroyed.
Brahmanand says: He crosses over the ocean of samsara.

RACHAA PRABHO

RAGA - Bhairavi TAL - Dadra

RACHAA PRABHO TUNE YAHA
BRAHMAA DA SAARAA
PRAANO SE PYAARAA
TU HI SABASE NYAARAA

1. TU HI MAATA TU HI TAATA
TU HI BANDHU TU HI BHRAATAA
SAKALA JAGATA ME EKA TERAA PRASARAA
RACHAA PRABHO....

2. MAHIMA TERE HAI APAARAA
KINHO NE NAHI PAYA PAARAA
BADE BADE GAYE HARA DHUNDA PHIRATA SAARAA
RACHAA PRABHO....

MEANING

The whole world is created by God.
I love you more than my life.
You are quite different from others.

1   You are my mother, you are my father,
You are my relative, you are my brother.
You are pervaded in this world.
The whole world was created by God.

2   Your glories are numberless.
No body could find out its end.
All great men have left after roaming and
trying to find that out.
Siva created this whole world.
How many people have sought
to know the power of God?
Although the great sages, the great yogis, holy men,
rishis and mahatmas have touched your power.
Only that one ultimate reality continues.
The whole world was created by God.

SANGATA SANTANA

RAGA - Pilu   TAL - Keherwa

> SANGATA SANTANAKEE KARA LE
> JANAMAKA SAADHANA KACHHU KARA LE

1. KAHAA SE AYAA KAHAA JAAYEGA
   IH KUCHH MALOOM KARANA RE BHAEE
   SANTANA KEE SHARANA JAKE BAABAA
   JANAMA MARANA DOOR KARA LE RE BHAEE

2. UTA MANAVA DEHA PAAYAA PRANEE
   ISAKA HITA KACHHU KARA LE RE BHAEE
   DO DIN KEE ZINDAGA NEE RE BANDHE
   HOSHIYAA RA HO KAR CHALANAA RE BHAEE

3. KAHATA KABIR SUNO BHAYEE SADHOO
   BAAR BAAR NAHEE AANA RE BHAEE
   AAPANA HITA KACHU KARA LAY PYAARE
   AAKHIRA EKALA JAANAA RE BHAEE

MEANING

Oh Brother, always keep the company of Saints,
Do some Sadhana in your life.
(spiritual discipline for self unfoldment and God realization).

1 Oh Brother, find out where did you come from and
   where are you going?
   Surrender to the lotus feet of the Saint (Guru),
   and be free from this cycle of birth and death.

2 Oh Brother you have earned this human body.
   Do something meritorious for yourself.
   You are only here for a few days.
   Remember this and walk carefully on your path.

3 Oh seeker, Kabir says: Listen fellow souls,
   Do not come again and again.
   Do something good for yourself and practise Sadhana.
   After all, you have to go alone.

SAADHO MANKAA

RAGA - Darbari Kanada   TAL - Tintal

SAADHO MANKAA MAAN TYAGO
SAADHO MANKAA MAAN TYAGO AAA
KAAMA KRODH SANGATA DURAJANA KEE
INSE AHANISI BHAAGO SAADHO MANKA....AAAA

1. SUKH DUKH DONO SAMA KAR JANO
   OUR MAAN APAMAANAA
   HARSHA SHOK SE RAHE ATEETAA
   TEENA VO TATWA BACHAANAA
   SAADHO MANKA...AAAA

2. ASTUTI NINDAA DONO TYAAGO
   JOE HAI PARAMA PADA PAA NAA
   JAN NAANAK YAHA KHEL KATHIN HAI
   SAD GURU KE GUNA GAANAA SAADHO

MEANING

Oh good man, leave the ego behind.
Give up lust, anger and bad company.
Guard against them every moment.

1 Happiness and unhappiness must be regarded equally.
   So also are honor and dishonor, pleasure and grief,
   all the pairs of opposites.
   Free yourself from karma that binds you to samsara.
   Only three elements should be saved.

2 Guru Nanak says, give up praise and blame
   even though it is very dificult.
   Sing the glories of the Sad Guru.

TUMAKA CHALATA RAAMACHANDRA

RAGA - Pilu   TAL - Dadra

TUMAKA CHALATA RAAMACHANDRA
BAJATA PAI JANIYA

1. KILAKI KILAKI UTHATA DAIYA
   GIRATA BHOOMI LATA PA TAI
   DHAI MATA GOAD LAIT
   DASHARAT KEE RAANIYA

2. ANCHALA RAJA ANGA JHARI
   BIBIDHA BHAATI SO DULAARI
   TAN MAN DHAN VAARI VARI
   KAHA TA MRIDU BACHANIYEA

3. BIDRU MA SE ARUNA ADHARA
   BOALLATA MUKHA MADHURA MADHURA
   SUBHA GANA SE KAME CHARU
   LATA KATA LATA CHA NIYA

4. TULSIDAS ATI ANANDA
   DEKHI TAY MUKHAARABINDA
   RAGHU WARA CHABI KAY SA MAN
   RAGHU WARA CHABI BANIYEA

MEANING

Shri Ramachandra is walking dancingly.
The little bells of his anklets are jingling.

1   Smilingly he gets up and tumbling he falls down.
    His mother, running,takes him in her lap.

2   Dasharat's queens take little Rama in their laps and
    their saris become dusty.
    They love him with their body, their mind and soul (inner wealth)
    they talk to him softly.

3   With his coral red lips he speaks sweet words.
    Between his beautiful nose the nose ring is hanging.

4. Tulsidas is extremely happy by seeing the lotus flower face of Rama.
    Tulsidas says that Rama's picture is very similar to Rama's face.

GURU MANTRAS

OM NAMO BHAGAVATE SIVANANDAYA

HYMNS TO THE GURU

1. BRAHMAANANDAM PARAMASUKHADAM
   KEVALAM JNANAMOORTIM
   DVANDVAATEETAM GAGANA SADRISHAM
   TATVAMASYAADI LAKSHYAM
   EKAM NITYAM VIMALAM ACHALAM
   SARVADHEE SAAKSHIBHOOTAM
   BHAAVAATEETAM TRIGUNA RAHITAM
   SAT GURUM TAM NAMAAMI

2. CHAITANYAM SHAASWATAM SHAANTAM
   NIRAAKAARAM NIRANJANAM
   NAADA BINDU KAALAATEETAM
   TASMAI SREE GURAVE NAMAH

3. GURUR BRAHMAA GURUR VISHNU
   GURUR DEVO MAHESHWARAH
   GURU SAAKSHAAT PARAMBRAHMA
   TASMAI SREE GURAVE NAMAH

4. AJNAANA TIMIRAANDHASYA
   JNAANAANJANA SHALAAHKAYAA
   CHAKSHUR UNMEELITAM YENA
   TASMAI SREE GURAVE NAMAH

5. DHYAANA MOOLAM GUROR MOORTIH
   POOJA MOOLAM GUROH PADAM
   MANTRA MOOLAM GUROR VAAKYAM
   MOKSHA MOOLAM GUROH KRIPAA

6. OM NAMAHSHIVAAYA GURAVE
   SATCHIDANANDA MOORTAYE
   NISHPRAPANCHAAYA SHAANTAAYA
   SREE SIVANANDAAYA TE NAMAH
   OM SREE VISHNUDEVANANDAAYA TE NAMAH

MEANING

(See Satsang 2 Page 65)

SREE GURU BHAJAN

GARLAND OF RAGAS - Bheempalas, Jaunpuri, Bahar, Patadip, Dhani
TAL-Keherwa

BHEEMPALAS

JAY GURU DEV DAIYANI DEV BHAKTANA KE HITAKAAR
SIVAANANDA JAY MOHAVINAASHAKA BHAVABANDHANA HAREE

JAUNPURI

SIVANANDA JAI
S N D P M P / N N D P M P / G / R S / R R S /
S R / M P / D D P M / P N / D P / M P / N S / P N S
SIVAANANDA JAY MOHA VINAASHAKA BHAVABANDHANA
HAAREE / BHAKTANA KE HITAKARI
JAY GURU DEV....

BAHAR

BRAHMAA VISHNU SADAA SIVA KAA
S / D N P M P / G / G / M R S / N S M G / M P / G / G / M R S
/ N S / M G / M P / G M / N D / N S / D N S / D N S
BRAHMAA VISHNU SADAA SIVA KAA

PATADIP

GURUMURATI DHAAREE
S N D P M P / N N D P M P / D P M P / G M P / G M G R S /
G R S M G R S / P M G R S / N S G M P N / S N D P M P/G M P N S
GURUMURATI DHAAREE

BHEEMPALAS

VEDA PURAANA KAHATA BAKHAANA
P / M P / G M / P N / D P / M P / G M P / G M G R S /
G R S M G R S / P M G R S / N S G M P / M P G M P M P
VEDA PURAANA KAHATA BAKHAANA

DHANI

GURU KI MAHIMA BHAAREE
S N D P M G R S / S R G S R N S /
R S / G R / M G / P M / D P / N D / S N / R S / N D P M G R S
S R G S R N S / R M P N D P M P / R M P D P M P
GURU KI MAHIMAA BHAAREE
BHAKTANA KE HITAKAAREE
JAY GURUDEV...

JAPA TAPA TIRATHA SHAMA YAMA DAMA
GURU BINA NAHI HOVATA GYAANA
GYAANAKHARGA SE KARMA KATE
GURU NAAM SABA PAAPA KI HARI
BHAKTA NA KE HITAKAAREE

TAN MAN DHAN SAB ARPAN KEEJAY
PARAMA GATI MOKSHA PADA KIJE
SABA KE SARA SADAA GURU NAAMA
AVINAASHI ADHIKAREE
BHAKTANAKE HITAKAAREE

MEANING

1. Victory to Guru who is full of mercy, the benefactor of his devotees.
    Victory to Sivananda the destroyer of attachments,
    breaker of the shackles of material life.

2. Guru is the embodiment of Brahma, Vishnu and Sada Siva.
    The Vedas and Puranas describe great praises of Guru.

3. Chanting, penance, pilgrimage or knowledge,
    yoga and wisdom cannot be obtained without Guru.
    The sword of knowledge destroys karmas.
    The name of Guru destroys all sins.

4. Devote body, mind and wealth.
    Obtain salvation.Gurus name is the essence of everything.
    He is the Eternal Lord. He is the benefactor of devotees.

CHANT

OM NAMO BHAGAVATE SIVAANANDAAYA

SIVAANANDA PAHI MAAM SIVAANANDA RAKSHA MAAM
SATGURU DEVA PAHI MAM SATGURU DEVA RAKSHA MAAM

JAYA GURU DEV JAYA JAYA GURU DEV
JAYA GURU DEV JAYA SIVAANANDA
JAYA GURU DEV VISHNUDEVAANANDA
JAYA GURU DEV NADABRAHMAANANDA
JAYA GURU DEV SWAAMEE CHIDAANANDA

DEVA DEVA SIVAANANDA

RAGA - Gandhari   TAL - Dadra

1. DEVA DEVA SIVAANANDA
   DEENABANDHO PAAHI MAM
   CHANDRAVADANA MANDAHAASA
   PREMAROOPA RAKSHA MAAM
   MADHURA GEETA GAANALOLA
   JNANAROOPA PAHI MAAM
   SAMASTALOKA POOJITAANGA
   MOHANAANGA RAKSHA MAAM

2. DIVYA GANGAA TEERAVAASA
   DAANASHEELA PAHI MAAM
   PAAPAHARANA PUNYASHEELA
   PARAMAPURUSHA RAKSHA MAAM
   BHAKTALOKA HRIDAYAVAASA
   SWAMEENAATHA PAHI MAAM
   CHITSWAROOPA CHIDAANANDA
   NAMAH SIVAAYA RAKSHA MAAM

MEANING

1 Sivananda is God of gods,
   brother of the humble - may he protect me.
   Moon like face, mild smile,
   embodiment of love, may he protect me.
   Who delights in singing sweet songs,
   embodiment of wisdom may he protect me.
   Who is adored by all beings,
   who is of charming limbs, may he protect me.

2. Who resides by the bank of the river Ganga,
   who is generous, may he protect me.
   Who removes sin, who is full of virtues,
   Supreme Purusha, may he protect me.
   Who abides in the hearts of the devotees,
   the Lord may he protect me.
   Who is the embodiment of consciousness and bliss,
   salutations to Siva, may he protect me.

DHIRE DHIRE JAA

RAGA MALA - Khambavati, Chand, Bhairavi   TAL - Keherwa

DHIRE DHIRE JAA RAHI DHIRE DHIRE JAA

1. MUKTIKAA MARGA HAI RE TALAVAARA KI DHAAR
   SAMBHALA SAMBHALA KARA JAA
   DHIRE DHIRE JAA RAAHI DHIRE DHIRE JAA
   RAAHI DHIRE DHIRE JAA

2. KANKARA PATHARA SE KABHI NA HI DARANA
   KADAMA KADAMA PARA MANZIL KO CHALANA
   SANSAARKE ULJHANSE JABA GHABARAATE
   SADGURUKE CHARANOMEN JAA
   DHIRE DHIRE JA RAAHI DHIRE DHIRE JAA

RAGA SHIVARANJANI

3. KAALE KAALE BAADALONKE
   GHANA GHATA CHHAI
   GHANA GHATA CHHAI
   KAALE KAALE BAADALONKE
   S R G G R G R S / D S P D S S

   KAALE KAALE BAADA LONKE
   S R G P / R G P D / G P D S / P D S
   P D S R G R S D R S D P G R S
   S R G P D S R G R S D P G R S

   KAALE KAALE BAADALONKE
   S R G G R G R S / R G P P G P G R
   G P D D P D P G / P D S S D S D P
   P D S R G R S D R S D P G R S .
   KAALE KAALE BAADALONKE

RAGA BHAIRAVY

4. DOORA HAI NAGARI TERE
   LAMBHI CHARHAYE
   LAMBHI CHARHAYE

   DURA HY NAGARE TERE
   P / M P / D P / M P / N D P M G R S

   DURA HY NAGARE TERE
   S R G M P / M P D P M P N D P /
   M P D N S N D P M P N D P M G R S

DURA HY NAGARE TERE
S R G M P D N S / S R G R S N D P

DURA HY NAGARE TERE
LAMBHI CHARHAYE

5. SWAAMEE SIVAANANDA TUJE
   SWAAMEE SIVAANANDA TUJE
   RAHA BATALAYENGE
   SWAMEE SIVAANANDA TUJE
   JOTI DHIKHALAYENGE

6. NAADABRAHMAANANDA GITA GAATE GAATE JAA
   SAMBHALA SAMBHALA KARA JAA

   DHIRE DHIRE JAA RAAHI DHIRE DHIRE JAA

MEANING

1 Walk carefully O traveler, go slowly.

2 Do not ever be afraid of little or big pebbles.
   Make every step your goal.
   When you are confused by worldly matters
   take the shelter in Guru's feet.

3 Black clouds are heavily spread.

4 Your city is far.
   You have to walk a long distance.

5 Swami Sivananda will guide you to the right path.
   Swami Sivananda will show you the light.
   He will show you the path.

6 Go singing the songs of Nadabrahmaananda.

GANGAA KINARE

RAGA - Kambavati   TAL - Keherwa

1. GANGAA KINARE MERA DERA
   ANANDA KUTIRA MEN VAASA HAMAARAA
   SWARGA ANANDA KUTIRA
   KASHA AVATANA DHAARAA SWAMEE SIVAANANDA
   GURUVARA POOJYA HAMARA
   GANGAA KINARE.....

2. KALA CHALA KALA CHALA
   GANGAA CHALATA HAI
   BAHATA SUSITALA MERA
   GANGAA KINARE MERA DERA....

3. SUNDARA BADANA
   SUMADHURA VACHANA
   HOWATA SIVAANANDA MERA
   DESH VIDESHA SE BHAKTA PADHAARE
   MILANA SWAMEE YOGI MERA
   GANGAA KINARE......

4. JAGA ME GYAN KE GANGAA BAHAANE
   MAANAVA JEEVAN DIVYA BANAYE
   SWAMEE SIVAANANDA CHARANA KAMALA MEN
   NAADA BRAHMA BASAAYAA . GANGAA KINARE.....

MEANING

1. My hut is on the bank of the Ganges.
   I live in the hut of happiness. My little hut is like heaven.
   I am blessed to have as my Guru Master Sivananda
   who wears the orange robe and is a great Yogi.
   This worshipful Guru is revered by all.

2. With rippling sound, the Ganges is flowing.
   My heart is flowing in happiness.
   My hut is on the bank of the Ganges.

3. My Sivananda has a beautiful body.
   Whatever he speaks is very sweet.
   From this and other lands the devotees come to meet my Yogi Swami.

4. He spread the knowledge in the world.
   He made the life of humans divine.
   At the lotus feet of Swami Sivananda, Nadabrahmananda stays.

PARAVATA PE HAI SOHAANAA

RAGA - Tilaka Kamod   TAL - Keherwa

> PARAVATA PE HAI SOHAANAA
> SIVAANANDA KA DARBAAR
> DARSHANA KAA HAI NAJAARAA

1. SAB RISHI MUNI YE KAHATE HAI
   UPKAAR TUMA KAMAALO
   MANUSH JANAMA AMOLAKA
   ISAKO NA TUM GAWAALO
   HIRAJANAMA AMOLOKA
   MANUSH JANAMA AMOLOKA
   MILEGA NAHEE DUBAARAA
   DARSHAN KA HAI NAJARA.
   PARAVATA PE HAI.......

2. BHARAT TO KYA VIDESHOME
   ISAKA PRACHAARA BHAARI
   SIVAANANDAJI KO HAI POOJE
   YAHA DUNIYA AJA SAARE
   BRAHAMAANANDA KAHAI DUVAARAA
   NADABRAHMANANDA KAHAI DUVAARAA
   GITO KA HAI BHANDARA
   DARSHAN KA HAI NAJARA

MEANING

On the mountain is beautiful Sivananda's court.
The sight seems like a gift of God.

1   All seers and sages say that
you earn merits by doing good to others.
Human birth is precious. Don't waste it.
Human birth is the most precious treasure,
You won't get it again.

2   His name is popular in Bharat (India)
as well as other countries.
All this world is worshipping Sivananda.
Brahmanand says it again that these songs are like a treasure.
Oh the sight of Sivananda's court seems like a gift of God.

AANANDA KUTIRA

RAGA - Patmanjari   TAL - Keherwa.

1. AANANDA KUTIRA KE DIVYA DEVATAA
   SIVAANANDA SADAA AMARA RAHE
   AKHILA VISHWA KAA DIPTA SITAARAA
   BHAARATA JYOTI JALATE RAHE

2. PREMA BHAKTI KAA DEEPA JALE
   HAME JAAGRATI KE AURA RAAHA MILE
   MAANAVA DUKHA MITAA TE RAHE
   SIVAANANDA SADAA AMARA RAHE
   JALA TE JAGAME SHAANTI NIRAALI
   JNYANA SADA BARASAATE RAHE
   AANANDA KUTIRA....

3. SIHVA SHANKARAKA LE AVATAAR
   DAYAA PREMA KAA HAI BHANDAAR
   JAGA KO DIVYA BANATE RAHE
   SIVAANANDA SADA AMARA RAHE
   SANKATKE PATHASE DOORA KIYE
   HAME SATYA MARGA DIKHALATE RAHE
   AANANDA KUTIRA...

4. MUKHAME HARI KAA GEETA RAHE
   AURA SIVA KE CHARANA ME PREETA RAHE
   AMRITA GITA SUNATE RAHE
   SIVAANANDA SADA AMARA RAHE
   ISA DHARATEE PARA YUGA YUGA SWAMI
   NAADABRAMAA BARASATE RAHE
   AANANDA KUTIRA....

MEANING

1   Magnificent Devata (Lord) of the cottage of bliss.
    May Sivananda be immortal forever.
    Shining star of the whole world.
    May the light of Bharat (India) stay lit.

2   Let the lamp of love and devotion kindle
    Lead us to the path of awakening and
    destroy humanities pains.
    May Sivananda be immortal forever.
    He showers knowledge.
    There is incomparable peace in the burning world.

3   Manifesting as Shiv Shankar,
    full of compassion and love.
    May he keep making the world magnificent.
    May Sivananda be immortal forever.
    He has removed all obstacles and
    shows us a path of truth.

4   May there be the song of Hari (Krishna)
     on the lips and love in the feet of Shiva.
    May he narrate the immortal Gita.
    May Sivaananda be immortal forever.
    May He shower the sound of Brahman on this earth for ages.

**JAYA GURUDEV JAYA JAYA GURUDEV JAYA
JAYA GURUDEV JAYA SIVANANDA GURU JAYA**

ADORATIONS TO RAAMA

SREE RAAMA STOTRAM

RAGA - Desh   TAL - Keherwa

MANGALAM RAAMACHANDRAAYA
MAHANEEYA GUNAABDHAYE
CHAKRAVARTEE TANUJAAYA
SARVABHAUMAAYA MANGALAM
MANGALAM SATYAPAALAAYA
DHARMA SAMSTHITI HETAVE
SITAAMANOBHIRAAMAAYA
RAAMACHANDRAAYA MANGALAM

MEANING

May auspiciousness be to Lord Ramachandra,
Who is an ocean of great qualities,
Who is the son of an emperor (Dasaratha)
Who Himself is an emperor, to Him be auspiciousness.
May auspiciousness be to the protector of Truth,
Who is the cause for the firm establishment of virtue (Dharma)
Who is the delight of Goddess Sita's mind,
May auspiciousness be to that Rama.

SREE RAAM JAYA RAAM

SREE RAAM JAYA RAAM JAYA JAYA RAAM (8X)
SHUDDHA BRAHMA PARAATPARA RAAM
KAALAATMAKA PARMESHWARA RAAM
SESHA KALPA SUKHA NIDRITA RAAM
CHANDRA KIRANA KULA MANDANA RAAM
SREEMAD DASARATHA NANDANA RAAM
KAUSALYA SUKHAVARDHANA RAAM
VISHVAAMITRA PRIYADHANA RAAM
GHORA TAATAKA GHAATAKA RAAM
MAAREECHADI NIPAATAKA RAAM
KAUSIKA MAKHA SAMRAKSHAKA RAAM
SREEMAD AHALYODDHARAKA RAAM
GAUTAMAMUNI SAMPOOJITA RAAM
SURAMUNIVARAGANA SAMSTUTA RAAM
NAAVIKA DHAAVITA MRIDUPADA RAAM
MITHILAAPURA JANA MODAKA RAAM
VIDEHA MAANASA RANJAKA RAAM
TRYAMBAKA KAARMUKA BHANJAKA RAAM
SEETARPITA VARAMAALIKA RAAM
KRITA VAIVAHIKA KAUTUKA RAAM
BHAARGAVA DARPA VINAASHAKA RAAM
SREEMADAYODHYAPAALAKA RAAM
RAGHU PATI RAAGHAVA RAAJAA RAAM

PATITA PAAVANA SEETA RAAM
ISHVARA ALLA TERE NAAM
SABAKO SANMATI DE BHAGAVAAN

MEANING

Pure, supreme Brahman, and without attributes, is Rama.
Embodiment of time, Supreme Lord is Rama.
Blissful sleeper on the bed of Sesha (the lord of serpents) is Rama.
Worshipped by Brahma and other gods is Rama.
The adornment of the solar race is Rama.
The son of great Dasaratha is Rama.
The increaser of the delight of Kausalya is Rama.
The coveted treasure of Vishvamitra is Rama.
The destroyer of terrible Tataka is Rama.
The slayer of Mareecha and other demons is Rama.
The protector of the sacrifice of Vishvamitra is Rama.
The uplifter of Ayodhya is Rama.
The Lord worshipped by Gautama is Rama.
Who is praised by gods and great sages is Rama.
Whose feet were washed by the boat man (Guha) is Rama.
Who charmed the people of Mithilapuri is Rama.
Who broke the bow of Siva, the three-eyed, is Rama.
Who was garlanded (in marriage) by Sita is Rama.
Who is happy and joyful about his marriage (with Sita) is Rama.
Who destroyed the pride of Parasurama is Rama.
Who sustained Ayodhya is Rama.
O Lord of Raghu dynasty, born in the line of Raghus,
Purifier of the fallen,
O Sitarama, Ishvara and Allah are thy names.
Give virtous mind to all.

KHELATI MAMA HRIDAYE

RAGA - Bhoopa   TAL - Keherwa

SHLOKA

JAYATU JAYATU MANTRAM
JANMASAAPHALYA MANTRAM
JANMA MARANA BHEDA KLESHA
VICCHEDA MANTRAM
SAKALA NIGAMA MANTRAM
SARVA SHAASTRAIKA MANTRAM
RAGHUPATI NIJA MANTRAM
RAAMA RAAMETI MANTRAM

MEANING

Victory, victory to that Mantra
which makes the human birth fruitful,
The Mantra that cuts at the root of
All afflictions of births and deaths,
The Mantra of all Vedas and Sastras.
Lord Rama's own Mantra
The Mantra of Ram Ram.

BHAJAN

KHELATI MAMA HRIDAYE SREE RAAMA
KHELATI MAMA HRIDAYE SREE RAAMA

1 MOHAMAHAARNAVA TAARAKAKAAREE
   RAAGA DWESHA MUKHASURAMAREE

2 SHAANTI VIDEHASUTAA SAHACHAREE
   DAHARAYODHYANAGARAVIHAREE

3 PARAMAHAMSA SAAMRAAJYODDHAREE
   SATYA JNANAANANDA SHAREEREE

MEANING

He plays in my heart, Rama plays in my heart.

1 He who takes one across the great ocean of Moha (ignorance)
   and destroys the Asuras, Raga and Dwesha.

2 He who has Shanti (repose) and the daughter of Videha (Sita)
   as his constant companion and
   who sports in the city of Ayodhya (the impregnable),
   which is Dahara (the eternal centre of the heart).

3 He who sustains the empire of the Parama Hamsas
   and whose form is Existence, Knowledge and Bliss.

NAMAVALI

RAAMA RAAMA RAAMA RAAMA RAAMA NAAMA TAARAKAM
RAAMA KRISHNA VAASUDEVA BHAKTI MUKTI DAAYAKAM
JANAKEE MANOHARAM SARVALOKA NAAYAKAM
SHANKARAADI SEVYAMAANA PUNYA NAAMA KEERTANAM.

MEANING

The name of Rama is that which takes one across Samsara;
Ram, Krishna, Vasudeva are bestowers of devotion and liberation.
The delighter of Janaki's mind, the Lord of the whole universe.
Let us chant the holy name of the Lord who is worshipped by Shankara.

PIBA RE RAAMARASAM

RAGA - Malkouns   TAL - Adital

SHLOKA

VAIDEHEE SAHITAM SURADRUMATALE
HAIME MAHAA MANDAPE
MADHYEPUSHPAKAM ASANE MANIMAYE
VEERASANE SAMSTHITAM
AGRE VAACHAYATI PRABHANJANASTUTE
TATTVAM MUNIBHYAH PARAM
VYAKHYAANTAM BHARATADIBHIH PARIVRITAM
RAAMAM BHAJE SHYAAMALAM

MEANING

I Worship Rama of blue complexion,
Who is seated in Veerasana with Sita,
On a seat of precious stones amidst flowers,
In the centre of a pulpit of gold,
Beneath the celestial tree;
In front of whom Hanuman is explaining
The supreme Tattwas (principles) to the sages;
Aand who is surrounded by Bharata and others.

BHAJAN

PIBA RE RAAMARASAM
RASANE PIBARE RAAMARASAM

1 DOOREEKRITA PAATAKA SAMSARGAM
   POORITA NAANAAVIDHA PHALA VARGAM

2 JANANA MARANA BHAYA SHOKA VIDOORAM
   SAKALA SHASTRA NIGAMAAGAMA SAARAM

3 PARIPAALITA SARASIJA GARBHANDAM
   PARAMA PAVITREEKRITA PAAKHANDAM

4 SHUDDHA PARAMA HAMSA ASHRAMA GEETAM
   SHUKA SAUNAKA KAUSIKA MUKHA PITAM

MEANING

Taste the nectar of Rama's name O my tongue.
Taste the nectar of Rama's name.

1 That which destroys the stains of sin
   and which abounds in various virtuous rewards.

2 That which dispels the fears and woes of birth and death;
   that which is the essence of all Sastras, Nigamas and Agam's.

3 That which protects all the worlds created by Brahma
   and which converts heretics into very holy men.

4 That which is sung (by Paramahamsas) in the hermitages of the holy Parama -ham-
   sas the nectar which is drunk by (the sages) Suka, Saunaka, Kausika and others.

RAAM RATAN DHAN PAYO

RAGA - Todi   TAL - Keherwa

> PAYO JI MAINAY
> RAM RATAN DHAN PAYO

1. VASTU AMOLAK DI MERE SATGURU
   KIRPA KAR APANAAYO
   PAYO....

2. JANMA JANMAKEE POONJI PAYI
   JAGME SABHI KHOVAYO
   PAYO....

3. KHARACHAI NAHI KOYI CHOR NA LOOTAY
   DIN DIN BARHAT SAVAAYO
   PAYO.....

4. SATKI NAAV KHEVATIYA SATGURU
   BHAVA SAGAR TARA AAYO
   PAYO.....

5. MIRAAKE PRABHU GIRIDHAR NAAGAR
   HARAKH HARAKH JAS GAAYO
   PAYO.....

MEANING

(See Bhajan 1 Pg 77)

BHAJA MAN RAAMA CHARAN SUKHADAAYEE

RAGA - Bhairavi   TAL - Keherwa

SHLOKA

POORVAM RAAMATAPOVANANI GAMANAM
HATVA MRIGAM KAANCHANAM
VAIDEHI HARANAM
JATAAYU MARANAM
SUGREEVA SAMBHAASHANAM
VAALEE NIGRAHANAM
SAMUDRATARANAM
LANKAAPURIDAAHANAM
PASCHAAD RAAVANA
KUMBHAKARNA MATHANAM
ETADDHI RAAMAAYANAM

MEANING

Beginning with Rama's going into the forests,
Then killing the golden deer,
Sita being carried away by Ravana,
Jatayu's death (being wounded by Ravana),
Talk with Sugriva,
Killing of Vaalee,
Crossing the ocean
Setting fire to Lanka by Hanuman,
afterwards Ravana
and Kumbhakarna meeting their end at the hands of Rama -
this is the story of Ramayana.

BHAJAN

BHAJA MAN RAAMACHARANA SUKHADAYEE

1   JIHI CHARANANSE NIKASI SURASARI
    SAANKAR JATAA SAMAYEE
    JATAA SANKARI NAAM PARYO HAI
    TRIBHUVAN TAARAN AYI

2   JIN CHARANANKI CHARAN PAADUKA
    BHARAT RAHYO LAV LAAYEE
    SOI CHARAN KEVAT DHOYI LINE
    TAB HARI NAAV CHALAYEE

3   SOYI CHARAN SANTANJAN SEVAT
    SADAA RAHAT SUKHADAYEE
    SOYI CHARAN GAUTAM RISHI NAARI
    PARASI PARAM PAD PAAYEE

4 DANDAKABAN PRABHU PAAVAN KINHO
   RISHIYAN TRAASA MITAAYEE
   SOYI PRABHU TRILOKAKE SWAAMEE
   KANAKMRIGAA SANG DHAAYEE

5 KAPI SUGRIVA BANDHU BHAYA VYAAKUL
   TIN JAYA CHAATRA PHIRAAYEE
   RIPUKO ANUJ VIBHISHAN NISHICHARA
   PARASAT LANKAA PAAYEE

6 SHIVA SANAKAADIKA ARU BRAHMAADIKA
   SESHA SAHASAMUKH GAAYEE
   TULSIDAAS MARRUT SUTAKI PRABHU
   NIJA MUKHA KARAT BADAAYEE

MEANING

Worship O mind, the Feet of Lord Rama, which bestow happiness.

1 From which Feet, started the heavenly Ganges
   and entered the matted locks of Sankara.
   Hence, She got the name Jata Sankari
   and came to enable people of the three worlds to cross the ocean of birth
   and death
   (Worship such Feet of Rama........)

2 On whose footware (Paduka) Bharata remained in meditation,
   whose Feet Guha washed and then rowed the boat of Hari
   (Worship such Feet of Rama......)

3 By serving those Feet, the saints ever remain as bestowers of happiness.
   By the touch of those Feet,
   Ahalya the wife of Rishi Gautama attained the Supreme State.
   (Worship such Feet of Rama.....)

4 The Lord purified the forests of Dandaka
   and removed the fears of the Rishis.
   That Lord is the Master of the three worlds.
   He gave liberation (Sayujya Mukti) to the golden deer (who was Maricha).
   (Worship such Feet of Rama.....)

5 By the grace of which Feet the monkey Sugriva
   though fear stricken from his brother (Bali) became ultimately victorious.
   By touching which Feet, enemy Ravana's brother
   Vibhishana Rakshasa got the kingdom of Lanka
   (Worship such Feet of Rama.....)

6 The Glory of which Feet, Siva, Sanaka, Brahma ,
   other Gods and Sesha with his thousand mouths sang,
   O Lord of the son of the Wind-God (Hanuman),
   Tulasidas, with his own mouth sings Thy glory.

AYE RAGHU VEERA DHEERA

RAGA - Malkouns   TAL - Dadra

AYE RAGHU VEERA DHEERA LANKA DESHA AVAAGA MANA
SANGA SAKHAA ANGADA SUGRIVA AURA HANUMAANA
RAHASA RAHASA GAAVATA YUVATE JAGABANDHANA
VEDAANAA
DEVAKUSUMA PARE KHATU GHANA JAAYE RAAHE NABHA
VEMAANAA

MEANING

Patient Rama has come. The conquerer of Lanka.
With him is his friend Angad, Sugriva and Hanuman.
Abandoning all their attachments the people are singing.
Devas are showering flowers Oh the protector of the world
Victory to You.

SHRI RAAMACHANDRA

RAGA - Malkouns   TAL - Rupak

(See Bhajan 2 Pg 81)

TARAANAA

TA NUM TA NA NA TA NA DAY RA NA-AA-AA
TA NUM TA NA NA TA NA DAY RAY NA-A
TANA DERE NA DHIM TUM
TA MUM TA NANA NANA NANA NANA NANA NANA
GRAN GRAN GRAN GRAN TA NUM TA NA NA TA NA DERE NA -
AA
PAJAGARA IDU SABHE GURASTAPAKI
GURASTANA MAMBU PARAWARA GI

MM/ NN/ DD/ MM/ NN/ DD/ NSS
MG/S/ ND/MG/S

KRAN DHA DHA DHIN NA TIRI KITA
DHA GI NA GI NAGA DHARA KITA TAKA
DHIRI KITA TAKA DHIRI KITA TAKA DHIN NA(3X)
DHA GI, TANUM TANANA TANA DERE NA.....

PREMA MUDITA

(See Satsang 1 Pg.39)

BARA SARASWATEE SA MA

RAGA - Gurjar Todi   TAL - Tintal

1. BARA SARASWATEE SAMAA GATA HO
   VIDYAA DAKE SARASA NIRASANAKO
   SAB JAGATA KO DEEJE GUNJANA KO
   BARA SARASWATEE SAMAGATA HO

2. RAAGA THAAT AURA TAALA SARASA HAI
   BACHA TA RE
   DEVEE DAYAA DAYINEE
   APANAY KAR SARASWATEE SA MA

MEANING

1. O Mother Saraswati come close to me.
   Giver of knowledge.
   Without you the world is dry.
   You make the world musical and sweet.

2. The ragas and talas cannot exist without your mercy.
   Please make me yours. Accept me
   Without your mercy I am nothing.

JAI JAI DEVI

RAGA - Darbari Kanada   TAL - Keherwa

SHLOKA

AMBAA SHAMBHAVEE CHANDRAMAULIRABALAA
APARNA UMAA PAARVATEE
KALEE HAIMAA VATEE SHIVAATRINAYANAA
KAATYAAYANEEBHAIRAVI
SAVITREE NAVAYAUVANAA SHUBHAKAREE
SAMRAJYALAKSHMEE PRADAA
CHIDROOPI PARAADEVATAA BHAGAVATEE
SREE RAAJARAAJESVAREE

MEANING

O Mother, consort of Lord Shambhu (Siva),
whose head is adorned with the crescent moon,
who is slim, who during Her penance gave up eating of even leaves,
Uma (who was urged not to resort to penance by Her parents),
Parvati (daughter of the mountain),
Kali (the terrible), Haimavati (daughter of Himavan),
Shivaa (consort of auspicious Siva), Three-eyed,
Katyayani (Durga), Bhairavi (consort of Lord Bhairava),
Savitri (Goddess of Gayatri Mantra, creatrix of the Vedas),
who is youthful, who is the giver of auspiciousness,
who is the bestower of prosperity of kingdoms,
who is in the form of wisdom, the supreme Goddess,
to that Sri Rajarajeswari I prostrate.

BHAJAN

JAY JAY DEVEE JAGAJANANEE MAA
SHARANAAGATA PARIPA ALINI MAA

1   DURGAA DURGATI NAASHINI MAATAA
    KALI KAAL VINAASHINI MAA
    JAYA JAG VANDINI TAARINI MAATAA
    MOOLADHAARAA NIVAASINI MAA

2   KAMALA NAYANE JAY MAA AMBAEE
    JAI JAG DHATRI MAA JAGADAMBAY
    EISHA NISHAREE JAY MAHESHWAREE
    JAGA TOH DHARINI JAY MAA AMBAEE

3   SHAKTIPRADAAYINEE DURGAA MAATA
    BHAKTI PRADAAYINEE DURGAA MAATAA
    JYNANAPRADAAYINEE DURGAA MAATAA
    MUKTIPRADAAYINEE DURGAA MAATAA

4   MAHABHAVAMAYEE JAYA MAA DURGE
    SATYASANAATINEE JAYA MAA DURGE
    BRAHMA SANAATINEE JAYA MAA DURGE
    PRAANA SVAROOPINEEJAYA MAA DURGE

5   JAYA MAA BHAVAANEE JAYA MAA SHIVAANEE
    JAG PAALANEE HAI JAGJANAANEE MAA
    VISHVA VILASINEE VISHVA VIMOHINEE
    VISHVAASA HAARINEE VISHVESWAREE MAA

MEANING

Glory to the Mother of the Universe

1 Durga destroys evils.
Kali destroys Yama (the God of death)
Salutations to the Mother who gives salvation to the world.
Glory to Mother, who lives in the origin of all creations.

2 Glory to the lotus eyed Mother Amba.
Glory to Mother Amba
who gives salvation to this universe.

3 Ma Durga, the giver of energy Ma Durga,
the giver of devotion.
Ma Durga, the giver of knowledge
Ma Durga is breath itself.

4 Mother Durga is everywhere.
Mother Durga is truth.
Mother Durga is Brahma.
Mother Durga is breath itself.

5 Glory to Bhavani Glory to Ma Shivani.
You protect this world.
You are the creator and also
the destroyer of the universe.
Glory to the Mother of the Universe.

BHAVAANEE DAYAANI

RAGA - Bhairavi   TAL - Jhaptal

1 BHAVAANEE DAYAANI
MAHAA VAAKAVAANEE
SURA NARA MUNI JANA DAANI
SAKALA BUDDHI JYNAANI
BHAVAANEE

2 JAGADJANANEE JAGA JAANEE
MAHISHAASURA MAR DINEE
UJWALA MUKHEE CHANDA
AMARA PADA JYNANI, BHAVAANEE

MEANING

1 Merciful Mother Bhavani.
Great Mother Vakavani.
You are the source of everyone's intelligence,
humans, devas, angels and sages.

2   Oh Mother the world has known you.
     Destroyer of Mahisasura (the evil demon).
     Moon faced Mother.
     You are the giver of immortal knowledge.

AADI DIVYA JYOTI MAHAA

RAGA - Bhairavi   TAL - Dadra

        AADI DIVYA JYOTI MAHAA
        KAALI MAA NAMAH
        MADHUSHUMBHAMAHISHAMARDINEE
        MAHAA SHAKTAYAY NAMAH
        BRAHMAA VISHNU SHIVA SWAROOPA
        TWAM NAA ANYATHAA
        CHARAA CHARASYA PAALIKAA
        NAMO NAMAH SADAA

MEANING

        (See Satsang 1 Pg 40)

SRI SARASVATEE STOTRAM

RAGA - Malkouns   TAL - Tintal

SHLOKA

        YAA KUNDENDU TUSHARAHAARADHAAVALA
        YAA SUBHRAVASTRAAVRITAA
        YAA VEENAA VARADANDA MANDITAKARAA
        YAA SHVETA PADMAASANAA
        YAA BRAHMAACHYUTA SHANKARA PRABHRITIBHIR
        DEVAIH SADAA POOJITAA
        SAA MAAM PAATU SARASVATEE BHAGAVATEE
        NISSHESHA JAADYAAPAHAA

MEANING

        May Goddess Saraswati,
        dispeller of all nescience and inertia,
        whose complexion is like jasmine blossoms, moon or snow,
        who is attired in spotless white sari,
        whose hands are adorned with enchanting Veena,
        who is always worshipped by Brahma, Vishnu, Siva and other Gods,
        who is seated in a white lotus, protect me.

SREE SARASWATEE NAMOSTUTE

RAGA - Malkouns TAL - Keherwa

SREE SARASWATEE NAMOSTUTE / VARADE VARADE
SREE SARASWATEE NAMOSTUTE / PARAA DEVATE

SRIPATI GAUREEPATI GURUGUHA VINUTE VIDHIYUVATE
SREE SARASWATEE NAMOSTUTE

1 VAASANAATRAYA VIVARJITA
   VARAMUNI BHAAVITA MOORTE
   VAASAVAADYAA KHILA NIRJARA
   VARAVITARANA BAHUKIRTE
   DARAHASA YUTAA MUKHAAMBURUHE /
   ADBHUTA CHARANAMBURUHE
   SAMSAARABHEETYAPAHE SAKALA
   MANTRAAKSHARA GUHE

MEANING

Salutations to thee, Sri Saraswati
Granter of boons   O Supreme Goddess
Saluted by Sripati (Vishnu), Gauripate (Siva),
Guru and Guha of Subramanya, darling of Brahma.

1 Free from the three types of Vasanas
   thy form is meditated upon by the best of saints.
   Thou art reputed for granting various boons to Indra and other Devas.
   O, Consort of Brahma with smiling face and wonderful lotus feet,
   the abode of all Mantras,
   and the dispeller of the afflictions of births and deaths.

VEENA PUSTAKA

RAGA - Bheempalas TAL - Keherwa

VEENA PUSTAKA DHAARINI AMBAA
VAANI JAYA JAYA PAAHI MAAM
SAAKTI DAAYINEE PAAHI MAAM
BHAKTI DAAYINEE PAAHI MAAM
BHAKTI DAAYINEE PAAHI MAAM
MUKTI DAAYINEE PAAHI MAAM

MEANING

O Mother, Goddess of learning, hail, hail to Thee.
O bestower of power, enjoyment, devotion and liberation.
Protect me from all evils and misfortunes.

DE MUJE DIVYAMATI

RAGA - Bheempalas   TAL - Rupak

SHLOKA

1   SARVAROOPAMAYI DEVI
     SARVAM DEVIMAYAM JAGATA
     ATOHAM VISHVAROOPAM TVAM
     NAMAMI PARAMESHVARAM

2   MANIKYAVEENAM UPALALAYANTIM
     MADALASAM MANJULAVAGVILASAM
     MAHENDRANILADYUTIKOMALAANGIM
     MATANGAKANYAAM MANASAA SMAARAMI

MEANING

1   Goddess is all forms. The whole world is full of Goddess.
     Therefore, O Parameswari (Goddess Supreme)
     of the form of all the worlds
     I prostrate to Thee.

2   I meditate on the daughter of Matanga Muni (Goddess Saraswati)
     Who is fondling (lovingly playing on) the Vina
      (an ancient musical instrument) bedecked with rubies,
     Who has beautiful gaits,
     Who is full of beautiful speech and
     Whose tender blue body shines like blue stone sapphire
     (Mahendra Nilam).

BHAJAN

     DE MUJE DIVYAMATI SARASWATEE
     DE MUJE DIVYAMATI

1.   RAMA KATHA BAHUGODA NIROOPANA
     CHALAVI SIGHRAGATI
     (DE MAAJAA....)

2.   BRAHMADIKA DEVA POOJATI TUJALA
     PRARTHANA HI KARITI
     (DE MAAJAA...)

3.   RAMADASA MHANE KAYA MALAA UNE
     TOO ASATA JAGATI
     (DE MAAJAA....)

MEANING

O Saraswati, give me intuition, give me intuition.

1   To relate the most sweet and excellent story of Lord Rama quickly,
     (give me intuition, O Saraswati).

2   Even Gods like Brahma worship and pray to you for it
     (give me intuition, O Saraswati).

3   Ramdas says: "I am never in want of anything when you are here".
     (O Saraswati, give me intuition).

DEENO DHAARINEE

RAGA - Bheempalas   TAL - Dadra

DEENO DHAARINEE DURITA HAARINEE
SATTWA RAJA TAMA TRIGUNA HAARINEE

SANDHYAA SAAVITREE SARASWATEE GAYATREE
SEETAA JAANAKEE PANKAJA LAKSHMEE
RAADHAA RUKMINEE PANKAJA LAKSHMEE
SEETAA JAANAKI PANKAJA LAKSHMEE

DEENO DHAARINEE DURITA HAARINEE
SATTWA RAJA TAMA TRIGUNA HAARINEE

MEANING

O uplifter of the humble and remover of sins.
Take away the three gunas, the three qualities of Sattwa (purity),
Rajas (activity) and Tamas (inertia, darkness).
You are Sandhya, Savitri, Saraswati,
Gayatri, Sita, Janake, Radha and Rukmini.
Oh Lotus flower Mother Lakshmi.

NAMAAVALI

GAUREE GAUREE GANGE RAJESHWAREE
GAUREE GAUREE GANGE BHUVANESHWAREE
GAUREE GAUREE GANGE MAHESHWAREE
GAUREE GAUREE GANGE MATESHWAREE
GAUREE GAUREE GANGE MAHAKALEE
GAUREE GAUREE GANGE MAHALAKSHMEE
GAUREE GAUREE GANGE PARVATEE
GAUREE GAUREE GANGE SARASWATEE

ADI DIVYA JYOTI MAHA   See Satsang 1 Pg. 40).

OM NAMAH SHIVAAYA   (Mantra) RAGA - Bheempalasi   TAL - Keherwa

BRAHMAMURAARI SURARCHITALINGAM

RAGA - Shivaranjani   TAL - Keherwa

SHLOKA

TASMAI NAMAH PARAMAKARAN KARANAAYA
DIPTOJJVALAJVALITAPINGALALOCHANAYA
NAGENDRAHARAKRITAKUNDALABHUSHANAYA
BRAHMENDRAVISHNUVARADAYA NAMAH SHIVAAYA

MEANING

I prostrate to Thee, who art the supreme cause of all causes,
Whose eyes are resplendent with purple colour,
Who hath earrings and otherornaments made of the garland of great serpents,
Who grants boons even to Lord Brahma, Indra and Lord Vishnu.
Namaha sivaya (Prostrations to Siva).

LINGASTAKAM (Eight verses on Lord Shiva)

1   BRAHMAMURAARISURARCHITALINGAM
    NIRMALABHAASHITASHOBHITALINGAM
    JANMAJADUHKHAVINAASHAKALINGAM
    TATPRANAMAAMI SADAASHIVALINGAM

2   DEVAMUNIPRAVARARCHITALINGAM
    KAAMADAHAM KARUNAAKARALINGAM
    RAAVANADARPAVINAASHANALINGAM
    TATPRANAMAAMI.......

3   SARVASUGANDHASULEPITALINGAM
    BUDDHIVIVARDHANAKAARANALIGAM
    SIDDHASURASURAVANDITALINGAM
    TATPRANAMAAMI.....

4   KANAKAMAHAAMANIBHUSHITALINGAM
    PHANIPATIVESHTITASHOBHITALINGAM
    DAKSHASUYAJNAVINAASHANALIGAM
    TATPRANAMAMI...

5. KUNKUMACHANDANALEPITALINGAM
    PANKAJAHARASUSHOBHITALINGAM
    SANCHITAPAAPAVINAASHANALINGAM TATPRANAMAAMI....

6. DEVAGANAARCHITASEVITALINGAM
   BHAAVAIRBHAKTIBHIREVA CHA LINGAM
   DINAKARAKOTIPRABHAAKARALINGAM   TATPRANAMAAMI....

7. ASHTADALOPARIVESHTITALINGAM
   SARVASAMUDBHAVAKAARANALINGAM
   ASHTADARIDRAVINAASHHANALINGA   TATPRANAMAAMI......

8. SURAGURUSURAVARAPOOJITALINGAM
   SURAVANAPUSHPASADAARCHITALINGAM
   PARAATPARAM PARAMAATMAKALINGAM   TATPRANAMAAMI......

MEANING

1   Lingam: the symbol of Lord Siva is adored by Brahma, Vishnu and all Gods. Taintless, shining, beautiful is Lingam; Destroyer of miseries that follow birth, is Lingam. I salute that Lingam of eternal Siva.

2   The Lingam (symbol) that is adored by the gods and great sages, that denotes the destruction of the God of lust, ocean of mercy, and the vanquishment of Ravana's pride - to that Lingam of the omnipresent Siva I prostrate.

3   The Lingam, that is anointed with fragrant materials like sandal paste etc. , the Lingam that enhances the intellect and that is worshipped by Siddhas, Gods and Asuras - to that Lingam.......

4   The Lingam that is adorned with jewels of gold and precious gems, that shines with the Lord of the serpents that encircles it, and that obstructed the sacrifice performed by Daksha - to that Lingam.........

5   The Lingam that is smeared with vermilion and sandal paste, that shines with garlands of lotuses and that dispels all the sins (of devotees) - to that Lingam......

6   The Lingam that is worshipped by Gods with great devotional feelings and that shines with brilliance of crores of suns - to that Lingam.....

7   The Lingam that is seated on an eight-petalled seat, that is the cause of all creations and that destroys eight kinds of destitution - to that Lingam.....

8   The Lingam that is worshipped by the preceptor of Gods (Brihaspati) and Gods, offering the flowers grown in the heavenly gardens and the Lingam that is the supreme Soul - to that Lingam....
    Whoever chants these eight verses in a Siva temple will attain Siva loka and will rejoice with Lord Siva.

HEY CHANDRAMAULI

RAGA - Shivaranjani   Tal - Jhaptal

HEY CHANDRAMAULI, HEY CHANDRASHEKAR
HEY SHAMBU TRILOCHANA
HEY SANKATVIMOCHANA
HEY TRIPURAARI SARJAKA

1   JAY JAY HEY SHANKAR HEY BHASMAANG SUNDAR
    HEY PASHUPATI HARIHAR
    HEY CHANDRAMAULI, HEY CHANDRASHEKAR

2   KANTHE DHARI CHHE TEN SARPONI MAALAA
    TAVA TANDAVE BAAJE DAMARU NIRAALAA
    TEN SHAILARAJE KITHU CHE DRADHAASAN
    TRINETRE KIDHUH RATIPATINUH VISARJAN

3   PRABHU VISHWA KAJE
    TEN SHIR GANGA DHAARI
    PARVATDUHITANI PUJA SHEEKAARI

4   JAG MANGALARTHE TE ASURA SANHAARYAA
    PI NE HALAAHAL TEN PATHA KAIN PRASAARYAA
    HEY CHANDRAMAULI, HEY CHANDRASHEKAR

MEANING

(Shankara's different names)
Hey Chandramauli, Hey Chandrashekar Hey Shankar, Three Eyed God,
Destroyer of obstacles, Creator of the three worlds.

1   Glory to such Lord Shiva, who shines with ashes on his body. Protector of
    animals.

2   You wear a snake garland on your neck,
    You dance with intricate drum beats. You the king of mountains have taken
    a firm sitting
    posture forever.   With your third eye you have killed Rati's husband
    Kamdeva (cupid God).

3   For the betterment of this world You have accepted Ganga on your head.
    Also you accepted the prayers of the daughter of Himalayas.

4   You have killed demons for the benefit of the world.
    You have drunk poison and shown many paths.

SHANKAR MAHAA DEVA DEVA

RAGA - Yaman   TAL - Jaleka

SHLOKA

SHAANTAM PADMAASANASTHAM SHASHADHARAMUKUTAM
PANCHAVAKRAM TRINETRAM
SHOOLAM VAJRAM CHA KHADGAM PARASHUMABHAYADAM
DAKSHINAANGE VAHANTAM
NAAGAM PASHAM CHA GHANTAM DAMARUKASAHITAM
CHAANKUSAM VAMABHAGE
NAANAALANKARADEEPTAM SPHATIKAMANIIBHAM
PARVATEESHAM NAMAAMI

MEANING

I prostrate before the five-faced Lord of Parvati, who is adorned with various ornaments, who shines like Sphatika jewel, who is seated peacefully in lotus pose, with mooncrested crown, with three eyes, wearing trident, Vajra, sword, axe on the right side,serpent, noose, bell, Damaru and spear on the left side and who gives protection from all fears to his devotees.

BHAJAN

SHANKAR MAHAADEVA DEVA SEVATA SABA JAAKE

1 JATAA MUKUTA SHISHAGANGAA / BAHATA TERI ATI PRACHANDA
GAURI ARADAANGASANGA / BHANGA RANGA SAAJE

2 DHYAAVATA SURA NARA MUNEESHA / GAAVATA GIRIJAAGIREE-SHA
PAAVATA NAHI PAARA SESHA / NETI NETI PUKAARE

3 BARANATA TULSIDAS / GIRIJAA PATI CHARANA AASHA
AISAA VARA VISHWANAATHA / BHAKTA HE PUKAARE

MEANING

Oh Shankar The great Deva, Everyone prays to you.

1 The long hair shines like a crown on your head and the forceful Ganga flows down. Mata Gauri sits and shines as the other half of your form.

2 Gods, men and Sages meditate on his name.Sing the glory of Girija and Girish.Sheshanag rests on his head calling,"Not this, Not this".

3 Tulsidas says: Lord of the Universe as your devotee all I am asking from you is the shelter at Lord Shankars feet.

NAMAAMI SAMISANA NIRVAANAROOPAM (Rudraastakam)

SHLOKA

AATMAA TVAM GIRIJA MATIH PARIJANAAH
PRANAAH SHARIRAM GRIHAM
POOJA TE VISHAYOPABHOGARACHA NAA
NIDRAA SAMAADHISTHITIH
SANCHAARAH PAADAYOH PRADAKSHINAVIDHIH
STOTRANI SARVA GIRO
YAD YAD KARMA KAROMI TATTADAKHILAM
SHAMBHO TAVAARADHANAAM

MEANING

O Lord Siva Thou art Atma or Soul,
my mind is Parvati, Thy consort,
the Pranas (vital airs) are Thy attendants,
my body is Thy abode enjoying
all the objects of the senses is Thy worship,
sleep is remaining in Samadhi (Superconscious State),
all walkings by my feet are perambulations to Thee,
all my words are Thy praises (hymns);
whatever actions I perform,
they are all acts of worship to Thee.

RUDRAASTAKAM (Eight verses on Rudra or Lord Siva)

1   NAMAAMISAMISANA NIRVAANAROOPAM
    VIBHUM VYAAPAKAM BRAHMAVEDASVAROOPAM
    AJAM NIRGUNAM NIRVIKALPAM NIRIHAM
    CHIDAKARAM AKASHAVAASAM BHAJEHAM

2   NIRAKARAM OMKARAMOOLAM TURIYAM
    GIRA JNANAGOTITAM ISHAM GIREESHAM
    KARAALAM MAHAAKAALAKAALAM KRIPAALAM
    GUNAGARASAMSAARAPAARAM NATOHAM

3   TUSHAARAADRISANKASAGAURAM GABHEERAM
    MANOBHOOTAKOTIPRABHAASWATSHAREERAM
    SPHURANMAULIKALLOLINICHAARUGANGA
    LASATPHALABALENDU KAANTHE BHUJANGA

4   CHALATKUNDALAM SHUBHRANETRAM VISHAALAM
    PRASANNAANANAM NEELAKANTHAM DAYAALAM
    MRIGAADHISHACHARMAMBARAM MUNDAMAALAM
    PRIYAM SHANKARAM SARVANAATHAM BHAJAAMI

5   PRACHANDAM PRAKRISHTAM PRAGALBHAM PARESHAM
    AKHANDAM BHAJE BHANUKOTIPRAKAASHAM
    TRYISHOOLANIRMOOLANAM SOOLAPANIM
    BHAJEHAM BHAVAANIPATIM BHAVAGAMYAM

6   KAALAATEETAKALYANAKALPAANTAKAARI
    SADAA SAJJANAANANDADAATAA PURAARIH
    CHIDAANANDASANDOHAMOHAPAHAARI
    PRASEEDA PRASEEDA PRABHO MANMATHAARIH

7   NA YAVAD UMANAATHAPADAARAVINDAM
    BHAJANTEEHA LOKE PARE VA NARAANAAM
    NA TAAVAT SUKHAM SHANTI SANTAPANAASHAM
    PRASEEDA PRABHO SARVABHOOTAADHIVAASA

8   NA JAANAAMI YOGAM JAPAM NAIVA POOJAAM
    NATOHAM SADAA SARVADAA DEVA TUBHYAM
    SARA JANMADUHKHAUGHATATAPYAMAANAM
    PRABHO PAAHI SAPANANAMAMEESHA SHAMBHO

9   RUDRASHTAKAMIDAM PROKTAM / VIPRENA HARATUSHTAYE
    YE PATHANTI NARA BHAKTYO
    TESHAAM SAMBHUH PRASEEDATA / ITI RUDRASTAKAM SAMPUR-
    NAM

MEANING

1 I adore you, the Lord and the Ruler of the whole universe, eternal bliss personified, the omnipresent and all pervading Brahma manifest in the form of the Vedas.
I worship Lord Siva, shining in his own glory, devoid of all attributes, undifferentiated, desireless, all pervading consciousness.

2 I bow to the Supreme Lord, who is formless, the source of Omkara, and the fourth state, beyond speech, understanding and sense perception, Ruler of Kailasa, devourer of even the Time spirit, terrible yet gracious, abode of virtues and extra cosmic.

3 I adore Him who is possessed of a form white as the snow clad Himalayas, radiant with the beauty of myriad cupids, whose head sparkles with the lovely stream of the Ganges, whose forehead is adorned by the crescent moon and neck coiled by serpent.

4 I adore the all merciful Sankara who has tremulous rings hanging from His ear lobes, who is possessed of beautiful eye brows and large eyes, who has a cheerful countenance and a blue speck on His throat, and who has a lion skin wrapped round his waist, and a garland of skulls round His neck.

5 I take my refuge in Bhavani's spouse, the supreme Lord, terrible, exalted, intrepid, indivisible, unborn and invested with the glory of myriad suns, who roots out the threefold agony and holds a trident in His hand, and who is accessible only through love.

6 Beyond part, ever blessed, bringing about universal destruction at the end of each round of creation, a source of perpetual delight to the virtuous, slayer of the demons Tripuras, consciousness and bliss personified, dispeller of delusion, be propitious my Lord, be propi-tious, destroyer of Cupid.

7 So long as men worship not the lotus feet of Uma's Lord, there is no happiness nor peace nor cessation of suffering for them, either in this world or in the next.
Therefore be propitious my Lord, dwelling as you do in the heart of all living beings.

8 I know not Yoga, nor Japa, nor rituals, I simply bow to You at all times, at every moment O Shambho. Pray protect me, my Lord, miserable and afflicted by sufferings attendent on old age and birth (and death) as I am, O Lord Shambho.

9 This hymn of eight verses was uttered by the Brahma in order to propitiate Lord Hara.
Sri Shambhu is pleased with those men who devoutly repeat it.

BHUKAN BHUGHANGA GHORA

SHLOKA

VANDE SHAMBU UMAPATI SURAGURU
VANDE JAGAT KARANAM
VANDE PANNA GA BHUSHANAM MRIGADHARAN
VANDE PASHUNAM PATIM
VANDE SURYA SHASHANKA VASHIYA NAYANAM
VANDE MUKUNDA PRIYAM
VANDE BHAKTA JANASHRAYAM CHAVARADHAM
VANDE SHIVAMSHANKARAM

MEANING

Glory to Shambu, UmaÕs husband, Glory to the Creator,
Glory to the Lord of all creatures,
Glory to him who gives solace to his devotees.

BHAJAN

1. BHUKHANA BHUGHANGA GHORA
   NIPATI SAKALA VADANA
   ARDHANGA GOURA
   SOHE VIBHUTA ANGA
   ARDHANGA GOURA

2. GALI RUNDAMALA HARE
   KHALAKO SHUBHAVASAN
   DAMARU GAIYO HATHA
   HARA RANG KARE NAMAN

3. CHAVAL CHANDHI SHIRA CHANDANA CHARHAY ANGA
   NANDIKI ASAVARI
   PYARI LAGE PARAM / ARAKA DHATURA
   PULANA BANI MAL / SHIVA SHIVA KARE CHATUR
   DHANA DHANA TRIPURA DHANA

   S/ N S R R S N P M / P/ N P
   M P N N P M P M P N S
   S/N S R R S N P M / P/ N P
   M P N N P M/ P M/ P N
   S N P M R M R S
   N S R M R S R M P N P M P N S
   N S R M R S N S N P M P N N S
   S N P M R M R S
   N S R M R S R M P N P M P N S

   BHUKAN BHUGHANGA GHORA / NIPATI SAKALA VADANA
   ARDHANGA GOURA / SOHE VIBHUTA ANGA
   ARDHANGA GOURA

1. A terrible snake. On his face all the snakes are wrapped around.
    Half of his body is white - Shakti Parvati.
    His whole body is smeared with ashes.

2. On his neck is Rudraksha mala and a garland of skulls.
    He has a drum in his hand. Everyone gives his salutations to that Lord.

3. We are offering him rice (rice on his head), chandan on his limbs.
    Rider of Nandi the bull. Parvati looks so beautiful with him.
    He wears the flowers of Dhatura (poisonous medicinal flower).
    Very intelligent people pray to Shiva and praise his greatness.

SAT SHRISTI TAANDAVA

BHAJAN

SAT SHRISTI TAANDAVA RACAITAA
NATA RAAJA RAAJA NAMO NAMAH
HAY AADYA GURU SHANKAR PITAA— NATARAAJ

1. GAMBHEER NAADA MRIDANGANAA
    DHABA KAY URAY BRAHMAANDA MA
    NITA HOTA NAADA PRACHANDANAA— NATARAAJ

2. SHIVA JNAANA GANGAA CHANDRAMAA
    CHID BRAHMA JYOTI LALAATAMAA
    VISHA NAADA MAALA KANTHAMAA—NATARAAJ

3. TAVA SHAKTIVAA MANGAY STHITAA
    HAY CHANDRIKAA APARAAJITAA
    CHAHU VEDA GAAYAY SANHITAA—NATARAAJ

MEANING

Adoration to the lord of the dancing art
The dancing form that brings joy
Oh eternal teacher, lord shankara
Adoration to thee

1. The beelike sound of the drum (mridangam)
    uplifts our consciousness from the world
    Daily this vibrating sound pervades everything

2. You posess vast wisdom like the vast ganga
    The brilliance of Brahma shines on your forehead
    You have the poisonous garland on your neck

3. We want your strength oh undefeatable one
    All the texts sing of thy glory. Adorations to thee

SIVA MAANASA POOJA (Mental Worship of Shiva)

1 RATNAIH KALPITAMAASANAM HIMAJALAIH
SNAANAM CA DIVYAAMBARAM,
NAANAARATNAA-VIBHOOSHITAM MRIGAMADAA-
MODAANKITAM CANDANAM.
JAATEE-CAMPAKA-BILVA-PATRA-RACITAM
PUSHPAM CA DHOOPAM TATHAA,
DEEPAM DEVA DAYAANIDHE PASUPATE
HRITKALPITAM GRIHYATAAM.

2. SAUVARNE NAVA-RATNA-KHANDA-RACITE
PAATRE GHRITAM PAAYASAM,
BHAKSHYAM PANCAVIDHAM PAYODADHIYUTAM
RAMBHAA-PHALAM PAANAKAM;
SAAKAANAAMA-YUTAM JALAM RUCIKARAM
KARPOORA-KHANDOJJVALAM,
TAAMBOOLAM MANASAA MAYAA VIRACITAM
BHAKTYAA PRABHO SVEEKURU.

3 CHATRAM CAAMARAYORYUGAM VYAJANAKAM
CAADARSAKAM NIRMALAM,
VEENAA-BHERI-MRIDANGAKAAHALAKALAA
GEETAM CA NRITYAM TATHAA;
SAASHTAANGAM PRANATIH STUTIRBAHUVIDHAA
HYETATSAMASTAM MAYAA,
SANKALPENA SAMARPITAM TAVA VIBHO
POOJAAM GRIHAANA PRABHO.

4 AATMA TVAM GIRIJAA MATIH SAHACARAAH
PRAANAAH SAREERAM GRIHAM,
POOJAA TE VISHAYOPABHOGARACANAA
NIDRAA SAMAADHISTHITIH;
SANCAARAH PADAYOH PRADAKSHINAVIDHIH
STOTRAANI SARVAA GIRO,
YADYATKARMA KAROMI TATTADAKHILAM
SAMBHO TAVAARAADHANAM.

5 KARACANAKRITAM VAAK KAAYAJAM KARMAJAM VAA,
SRAVANANAYANAJAM VAA MAANASAM VA APARAADHAM;
VIHITAM VIHITAM VAA SARVAMETAT KSHAMASVA,
JAYA JAYA KARUNAABDHE
SREEMAHAADEVA SAMBHO.

MEANING

1. Ocean of mercy, O Master of bound creatures, I have imagined a throne of precious stones for You, cool water for You to bathe in, divine robes adorned with many jewels, sandalwood paste mixed with musk to anoint Your body, jasmine, champaka flowers and bilva leaves, rare incense, and a shining flame. Accept all these which I have imagined in my heart for You, O God.

2. Sweet rice in a golden bowl inlaid with the nine jewels, the five kinds of food made from milk and curd, bananas, vegetables, sweet water scented with camphor, and betel leaves - I have prepared all these in my mind with devotion. O Lord, please, accept them.

3. A canopy, two yak-tail whisks, a fan and a spotless mirror, a vina, kettle-drums, a mridang and a great drum, songs and dancing, full prostrations, and many kinds of hymns - all this I offer You in my imagination. O almighty Lord, accept this, my worship of You.

4. You are my self; Parvati is my reason. My five pranas are Your attendants, my body is Your house, and all the pleasures of my senses are objects to use for Your worship. My sleep is Your state of samadhi. Wherever I walk, I am walking around You, everything I say is in praise of You, everything I do is in devotion to You, O benevolent Lord.

5. Whatever sins I have committed with my hands, feet, voice, body, actions, ears, eyes, or mind, whether prohibited by the scriptures or not, please forgive them all. Hail! Hail! O Ocean of compassion! O great God! O benevolent Lord!..-*

RAVANAKRITA SIVA TANDAVA STOTRAM

(Hymn On Siva's dance composed by Ravana)

SLOKA

SANTAM PADMASANASTHAM
SASADHARAMAKUTAM
PANCHAVAKTRAM TRINETRAM
SULAM VAJRAM CHA KHADGAM
PARASUMABHAYADAM
DAKSHINANGE VAHANTAM
NAGAM PASAM CHA GHANTAM
DAMARUKASAHITAM
CHANKUSAM VAMABHAGE
NANALANKARADIPTAM SPHATIKAMANINIBHAM
PARVATISAM NAMAMI

MEANING

Prostrate before the five-faced Lord of Parvati,
who is adorned with various ornaments,
who shines like Sphatika jewel,
who is seated peacefully in Lotus pose,
with moon-crested crown, with three eyes,
wearing trident, Vajra, sword, axe on the right side,
serpent, noose, bell,Damaru and spear on the left side
and who gives protection from all fears to his devotees.

TANDAVA STOTRAM

1 JATATAVIGALAJJALAPRAVAHAPAVITASTHALE
   GALEVALAMBYA LAMBITAM BHUJANGATUNGAMALIKAM
   DAMADDAMADDAMADDAMANNINADAVADDAMARVAYAM
   CHAKARA CHANDATANDAVAM TANOTU NAH SIVAM

2. JATAKATAHASAMBHRAMABHRAMANNILIMPANIRJHAREE-
   VILOLAVICHIVALLARIVIRAJAMANAMURDHAN
   DHAGA-DHAGA-DHAGA-JJVALALLALATAPATTA-PAVAKE
   KISHORACHANDRA-SEKHARE RATIH PRATIKSHANAM MAMA

3 DHARADHARENDRA-NANDINI-VILASA-BANDHU-BANDHURA
   SPHURADDIGANTA-SANTATI-PRAMODAMANA-MANASE
   KRIPA-KATAKSHA-DHORANI-NIRUDDHA-DURDHARAPADI
   KVACHID-DIGAMBARE MANO VINODAMETU VASTUNI

4 JATA-BHUJANGA-PINGALA-SPHURAT-PHANA-MANI-PRABHA
   KADAMBA-KUNKUMADRAVA-PRALIPTA-DIGVADHU MUKHE
   MADANDHA-SINDHURA-SPHURATTWAGUTTARAIYA-MEDURE
   MANO VINODAMADBHUTAM BIBHARTU BHOOTA-BHARTARI

5   SAHASRA-LOCHANA PRABHRITYASESHA-LEKHA-SEKHARA-
    PRASUNA-DHULI-DHORANI-VIDHUSARANGHRI-PITHABHUH
    BHUJANGA-RAJA-MALAYA NIBADDHA-JATA-JUTAKAH
    SRIYAI CHIRAYA JAYATAM CHAKORA-BANDHU-SEKHARAH

6   LALATA CHATVARA-JVALA-DDHANANJAYA-SPHULINGABHA-
    NIPITA-PANCHA-SAYAKAM NAMANNILIMPA-NAYAKAM
    SUDHA-MAYUKHA-LEKHAYA VIRAJAMANA-SEKHARAM
    MAHA-KAPALI-SAMPADE SHIRO-JATALA-MASTU-NAH

7   KARALA-PHALA-PATTIKA DHAGA-DDHAGA-DDHAGA-JJVALA-
    DDHANANJAYAHUTITKRITA-PRACHANDA-PANCHA-SAYAKE
    DHARADHARENDRA-NANDINI-KUCHAGRA-CHITRA PATRIKA-
    PRAKALPANAIKASILPINI TRILOCHANE RATIR-MAMA

8   NAVINA-MEGHA-MANDALI-NIRUDDHA-DURDHARA-SPHURAT-
    KUHUNISITHINITAMAH-PRABANDHA-BANDHA KANDHARAH
    NILIMPA-NIRJHARI-DHARA-STANOTU KRITTI-SINDHURAH
    KALANIDHANA-BANDHURAH SRIYAM JAGADDHURAN-
    DHARAH

9   PRAPHULLANILA-PANKAJA-PRAPANCHA-KALIMA-PRABHA-
    VALAMBIKANTHA-KANDALI-RUCHI-PRABHANDA-KANDHARAM
    SMARACHHIDAM PURACHHIDAM BHAVACHHIDAM
    MAKHACHHIDAM
    GAJACHHIDANDHAKACHHIDAM TAMANTAKACHHIDAM BHAJE

10 AKHARVA-SARVA-MANGALA KALAKADAMBA-MANJARI
    RASA-PRAVAHA-MADHURI-VIJRIMBHANA-MADHU-VRATAM
    SMARANTAKAM PURANTAKAM BHAVANTAKAM MAKHANTAKAM
    GAJANTAKANDHAKANTAKAM TAMANTAKANTAKAM BHAJE

11 AYATVADABHRA-VIBHRAMA-BHRAMAD-BHUJANGA-MAS-
    VASAD-
    VINIRGAMA-KRAMA-SPHURAT-KARALA-PHALA HAVYAYAT
    DHIMI-DHIMI-DHIMI-DDHVANAM-MRIDANGA-TUNGA-MAN-
    GALA-
    DHVANIKRAMA-PRAVARTITA-PRACHANDA-TANDAVAH SIVAH

12 DRISHAD-VICHITRA TALPAYOR-BHUJANGA-MAUKTIKASRAJOR-
    GARISHTHA-RATNA-LOSHTAYOR-SUHRID-VIPAKSHA-PAKSHAY-
    OH
    TRINARAVINDA-CHAKSHUSHOH PRAJAMAHI MAHENDRAYOH
    SAMA-PRAVRITTIKAH KADA SADA SIVAM-BHAJAMYAHAM

13 KADA NILIMPA-NIRJHARI-NIKUNJA-KOTARE VASAN
    VIMUKTA DURMATIH SADA SIRASTHAMANJALIM VAHAN
    VILOLA-LOLA-LOCHANO LALAMA-BHALA-LAGNAKAH
    SIVETI MANTRAMUCCHARAN KADA SUKHI BHAVAMYAHAM

14 IMAM HI NITYAMEVAMUKTAM UTTAMOTTAMAM STAVAM
    PATHAN SMARAN BRUVANNARO VISUDDHIMETI SANTATAM
    HARE GURAU SUBHAKTIMASU YATI NANYATHA GATIM
    VIMOCHANAM HI DEHINAM SUSANKARASYA CHINTANAM

15 PUJAVASANA-SAMAYA DASAVAKTRA GITAM
    YAH SAMBHU-PUJANA-PARAM PATHATI PRADOSHE
    TASYA STHIRAM RATHA-GAJENDRA-TURANGA-YUKTAM
    LAKSHMIM SADAIVA SUMUKHIM PRADADATI SAMBHUH

MEANING

1   May that Lord Siva graciously enhance my prosperity, the forest of matted
    hair on the crown of whose head is source of Ganga, and whose neck puri-
    fied by the flow of that holy stream is adorned with serpents as garlands,
    and who does His Tandava dance in tune with the sound of "Dam Dam"
    proceeding from his drum.

2   May I develop ever increasing devotion to Lord Siva, in the matted locks
    of whose head Ganga swiftly moves with her dancing waves, and the fire
    of whose forehead (Third Eye) burns with leaping flames with a sound like
    Dhaga, Dhaga, and on whose head the crescent moon sheds its lustre.

3   May my mind ever sport with that Digambara Tattwa (Lord Siva whose
    raiment is ether or consciousness), whose mind delights in the lustre shed
    by beauteous Girija (the daughter of Himalayas - Parvati), and by whose
    gracious look, even the greatest of miseries are averted.

4   May my mind be charmed by That Lord of Bhutas (spirits), on whose mat-
    ted locks the snakes spread their hoods, and yellow light that emanates
    from their gems adorns the faces of the damsels of the quarters with a ver-
    million glow, and who has put on a raiment of elephant's skin, and whose
    body is fair.

5   May he confer upon me everlasting wealth (of spirit) whose sandals are
    adorned with flower dust, fallen from the flowers of the crowns of Indra
    and other gods (while they bow to Lord Siva), and whose locks are
    adorned with the garland which is the King of snakes.

6   May that Siva enhance my prosperity, fire emanating from the altar of
    whose forehead destroyed god Cupid, who is adored by Indra, whose dia-
    dem shines by the light of the moon, whose forehead is broad, and head
    has matted locks.

7   May my mind be ever fixed on that Three-eyed Lord who offered Cupid as
    an oblation into the fire of His forehead, that burns with leaping flames,
    who as a master-artist adorns His consort Girija or Parvati.

8   May that Ganga-bearer Lord increase my prosperity, on whose neck there
    abides blackness of dark Amavasya (moonless) night, overcast by newly
    formed clouds; who has covered Himself with an elephant's skin, who

bears the burden of the entire universe and whose body glows like the moon.

9   I worship Him whose throat is as beauteous as a deer which has bluish glow of blue lotuses, and who is destroyer of Kama (god Cupid), Tripura (name of a demon), Bhava (Samsara-world), sacrifice of Daksha, elephant-demon Andhakasura, and Yama, god of Death.

10 I worship Him who like a black-bee enjoys the honey of the elegant beauty of prideless Parvati, and who is destroyer of Kama (god Cupid), Tripuras, Bhava, Daksha's sacrifice, elephant-demon Andhakasura, and Yama, god of death.

11 Glory to that Lord Siva, on whose head the terrible snakes moving very rapidly, emit hissing breaths, thus enhancing the fire of his forehead, and who dances in tune with the rumbling sound of Mridanga (drum).

12 When will I ever meditate on Siva, having possessed an equal vision between stones and velvety beds, snake and garland of jewel, precious gem and clod of earth, friend of foe, straw and beauteous damsels, common man and the emperor of the whole world.

13 When shall I be happy, chanting the Mantra of Siva with eyes streaming with tears of devotion, by the side of Ganga, in a solitary forest, keeping my hands folded on my head, absorbed in the thought of the moon-crowned Lord of beautiful forehead.

14 He who daily read this best of Stotras (praises), or remembers or describes it to others, ever remains pure, soon attains devotion to Siva, the preceptor of gods, never wanders from the righteous path, because devotion to Siva liberates all embodied beings.

15 In the evening, at the completion of one's worship, whoever reads this Siva Stotra, which was sung by Ravana, attains by the grace of Siva chariots, elephants, horses, wealth that abides forever.

SHANKARA TERE

RAGA - Shivaranjani   TAL - Jaleka

SHANKAR TERE JATAA MEN BAHATEE HAI GANGA DHARA
KAALI GHATAA KE ANDARA JIMIDAA MINI UJAARAA

1. GALE MUNDA MAALAA SAJE
   SASI BAALA ME BIRAAJE
   DAMARU NE NAADA BAAJE
   KARA MEN TRISULA DHAARAA

2. DRIGA TEENA TEJA RASI
   KATI BANDA NAAGA PHASI
   GIRIJAH SANGA DASI
   SABA VISHWA KE AADHAARAA

3. MRIGA CHARMA VASANA DHARI
   BRISA RAJA PAISA VAARI
   NIJA BHAKTA DUKHAHAARI
   KAILASA ME BIHAARAA

4. SHIVA NAAM JO UCHAARE
   SAB PAAP DOSA TARE
   BRAHMAA NANDA NABHI SARE
   BHAVASINDHU PARATAARE

MEANING

Oh Lord Siva the river Ganga flows from your matted locks.
It shines like a lightening in black clouds.

1   On his neck is a garland of skull, a
crescent moon is on his head. His drums
make a loud sound.In his hand is the trident.

2   His three eyes are full of light.
The serpent is wound on his hand. He
is Uma or Parvati's servant, Supporter
of the whole universe.

3   He who wears the deer skin rides on a bull.
Destroyer of the suffering of his true devotees.
He who is seated in Kailasa .

4   He who sings the name of Siva will have all sins destroyed.
Brahmanand says: He crosses over the ocean of samsara.

NAMO BHUTANAATHA

RAGA - Darbari Kanada   TAL- Keherwa

1. NAMO BHUTANAATHA, NAMO PARVATEESHA
   NARA RUNDHA MAALAA DHAARI
   VISHA SARPA TE SHAREERE
   DAMARU TRISHOOLA VAALAA
   KONI BHETAVE AMALA; NAMO.........

2. VYAAGHRA SANE VIRAJE
   LALAATA CHANDRA SAJE
   AVADHOOTA VESHA WAALAA
   KONI BHETAVE AMALA; NAMO......

3. SHOBHE JATETE GANGAA
   PIVO NIRAYI BHANGAA
   ALAMASTA BAILA WAALAA
   KONI BHETAVE AMALA; NAMO....

4. NACHE PISHYACHI SANGE
   JOBHI LINI SARANGE
   VAASA HOVE BHAWI KALA
   KONI BHETAVE AMALA; NAMO....

5. KARI SHANKHA NAADA RUNJE
   MUKHE RAMA NAMA GUNJE
   KSHANI JALI LE MADALA
   KONI BHETAVE AMALA; NAMO....

MEANING

1   Prostrations to the Lord of the Bhootas ,Lord of Parvati.He who wears the garland
    of skulls and poisonous snakes on his body.He holds the Damaru, the rhythm of
    creation and the Trishul, the symbol of the three gunas, the forces of creation.

2   Seated on a tiger,master of the senses,the moon shining on your fore-
    head.Who wears nothing but ash, symbol of complete renunciation. No
    one is better than you.

3   Ganga brings glory from the matted locks.He who drank the intoxicating
    drink and is always seated on his strong bull.

4   He dances in the company of spirits, becoming just like them.

5   He blows the conch, symbolizing the Nadam of creation.
    He sings Rama's name. He takes away all problems.

SHIVA AARTI

1   OM JAYA SHIVA OMKAARAA, PRABHU HARASHIVA OMKAARAA
    BRAHMAA VISHNU SADAASHIVA(2)
    ARADHAANGEE   DHAARAA...OMJAYA.

2   EKAANAN CHATURAANAN PANCHAANAN RAAJAY ,
    SWAAMI PANCHAANAN RAAJAY.
    HANSAASAN GARUDAASAN(2)
    VISHVAASAN RAAJAY...OM JAYA SHIVA OMKAARA

3. DO BHUJA CHAAR CHATUR BHUJA DASA BHUJA TAY SOYE,
    SWAAMEE DASA BHUJA TAY SOYE
    TEENO ROOPA NEERAKHATAA (2)
    TRIBHUVAN MANA MOHAY. OM JAYA SHIVA OMKAARA

4   YAKSHA MAALAA VANMAALAA MUNDMAALAA DHAAREE,
    SWAAMI MUNDMAALAA DHAREE
    CHANDAN MREEGHAMADA CHANDAA(2)
     BHOLAY SHUBHAKAAREE..OM JAYA SHIVA OMKAARA

5   SHVETAAMBAR PEETAAMBAR VYAAGHAAMBAR ANGAY,
    SWAMI VYAAGHAAMBAR ANGAY
    BRAHMAADIKA SANAKAADIKA(2)
     BHOOTADIKA SANGAY.OM JAYA SHIVA OMKAARA

6   KARAMADHYE CHA KAMANDAL CHAKRATRISHOOL DHARATAA,
    SWAMI CHAKRA TRISHOOL DHARATAA
    JAGAKARATAA JAGAHARTAA(2)
    JAGAPAALAN KARTAA OM JAYA SHIVA OMKAARA

7   BRAHMAA VISHNU SADAASHIVA MAANAT AVIVEKAA,
    SWAMI MAANAT AVIVEKAA
    PRANAVAAKSHARA KE MADHYE(2)
    YE TEENO EKAA.OM JAYA SHIVA OMKAARA

8   RIGUNA SWAMIJI KI AARATI JO KOEE JANA GAAVE
    SWAMI JO KOEE JANA GAAVE
    KAHATA SHIVAANANDA SWAMI(2)
     MANA VAANCHHIT PHAL PAAVE..OM JAYA SHIVA OMKAARA

MEANING

1   Victory to shiva the benevolent om, the remover of miseries.
    You are brahma, vishnu and the eternal Shiva.

2   You shine with one face, four faces, and five faces.
    The master shines with five faces.
    You are seated on the swan, the eagle and on the seat of the universe.

3   You sleep with two arms, four arms, and ten arms
    You are seen in the three forms, oh master of the three worlds.

4   You wear the yaksha garland, the vana garland, the munda garland.
    You always wear the sandal powder oh, performer of good deeds.

5   You wear white, yellow andclothes of the tiger.
    You keep the company of everyone.

6   You have a kamandalu in your hand and you carry the trishool wherever
    you go.
    Wou are the creator, the preserver, and the disintegrator of the world.

7   Those lacking in discrimination think you as brahma, vishnu, and sh\va.
    But the three are encompassed in the pranava letter om.

8   Swami Shivananda says those who sing the aarti of the great shiva
    will realize their desires in this life.

1. SHIVA SHIVA SHIVA
   SHANKAR ADI DEVA
   SHAMBHU BHOLA NAATH
   YOGI MAHA DEVA
   MAHA BALI SHIVA
   ADI ANTA SHIVA
   BHOOLANA SAKALA KAAJ
   HARA HARA MAHA DEVA

2. MAHA DEVA SHIVA SHANKAR SHAMBHU
   UMA KANTHA HARA TRIPURARI
   MRITUNJAYA VRISHABHA TRISHULA
   GANGA DHARA MRIDU MADANA HARE

3. SHIVA SHAMBHU / SHIVA SHAMBHU
   SHAMBHU SHANKARA NAMAH SHIVAYA
   SAAMBA SADAASHIVA NAMAHA SHIVAAYA
   KAILAASAVAASAA NAMAHA SHIVAAYA
   UMAA MAHEESHWARA NAMAHA SHIVAAYA
   SHAMBHU, SHIVA SHAMBHU...

4. SHIVAAYA PARAMESHWARAAYA
   CHANDRASHEKHARAAYA NAMAH OM
   BHAVAAYA GUNA SAMBAHAVAYA
   SHIVA TAANDAVAAYA NAMAH OM

5. JAI SHIVA SHANKARA BHUM BHUM HARA HARA
   HARA HARA / HARA HARA / HARA BOL HARAA
   SHIVA SHIVA SHIVA SHIVA / SHIVA AADI SUNDARAA
   HEY PARAMESHWARA DAYA KARO

6. HARA HARA MAHADEVA SHAMBHU
   KASHI VISWANAATHA GANGE
   HARA HARA MAHADEVA SHAMBHU
   KASHI VISWANAATHA GANG

7. SHAMBHU MAHAADEVA CHANDRA CHOODA
   SHANKARA SAAMBA SADAASHIVA
   GANGADHARA HARA KAILAASA VAASA
   PAHIMAAM PARVATIRAMANA
   SHIVAAYA SHIVAAYA SHIVAAYA NAMA H

HARAAYA HARAAYA HARAAYA NAMAH OM
NAMAH SHIVAAYA NAMAH SHIVAAYA

8. CHANDRSHEKHARAAYA NAMAH OM
   GANGA DHARAAYA NAMAH OM
   SHIVA SHIVA SHIVA NAMAH OM
   HARA HARA HARAYA NAMAH OM

9. DHIMIKA DHIMIKA DHIM / DHIMIKA DHIMIKA DHIM
   NACHE BHOLA NAATH / NACHE BHOLA NAATH
   MRIDANGA BOLE SHIVA SHIVA SHIVA OM
   DAMARU BOLE HARA HARA HARA OM
   VILA BOLE HARI OM HARI OM
   NACHE BHOLA NAATH / NACHE BHOLA NAATH

10. OM SHIVA OMKARA
    JAI JAI BAJE SHIVA OMKARA
    BRAHMA VISHNU SADAASHIVA
    HARA HARA HARA HAR MAHADEVA

11. JAI JAI SHIVA SHAMBHU
    JAI JAI SHIVA SHAMBHU
    MAHADEVA SHAMBHU
    MAHADEVA SHAMBHU

12 BOLE NAATHA UMAA PATE
   SHAMBHU SHANKARA PASHUPATE
   NANDI VAAHANA NAAGA BHOOSHANA
   CHANDRA SHEKHARA JATA DHARAA
   GIRIJAA RAMANA SADAASHIVA

13. NATARAAJ NATARAAJA
    SHIVANANDA NATARAAJA
    SHIVARAAJ SIVARAAJA
    SHIVANANDA SHIVARAAJA

14. SHAILA GIREESHWARA UMAA MAHESHWARA
    KAASHI VISHESHWARA SADAASHIVA
    SADAASHIVA, SADAASHIVA, SADAASHIVA SHAMBHU SADAASHI-
    VA

15. UMA PARVATI PATAYE HARA HARA
    HARA HARA SHANKAR MAHAA DEVAAYA
    OM SHIVA SHIVA SHIVA SAADASHIVAYA
    MAHAADEVAAYA SADAASHIVAYA

16. BOLO BOLO SAB MIL BOLO OM NAMAH SHIVAAYA
OM NAMAH SHIVAAYA OM NAMAH SHIVAAYA
JUTA JATA MEY GANGA DHARI
TRUSHUL DHARI DAMARU BAYAVEY
DUM DUM DUM DUM DAMARU BAAJE
GUNJUTHA OM NAMAH SHIVAAYA
OM NAMAH SHIVAAYA, OM NAMAH SHIVAAYA.....

MEANING

Chant together "Om Namah Shivaya
Lord Shiva with the holy river Ganges in his matted locks
and the trishula in his hand" plays the drum.
The echoes of "Om Namah Shivaya"
resonate throughout the whole universe

KRISHNA MANTRAS

1 OM NAMO BHAGAVATE VASUDEVAAYA

Om Salutations to Lord Krishna

2. MAHAA MANTRA

HARE RAAMA HARE RAAMA / RAAMA RAAMA HARE HARE
HARE KRISHNA HARE KRISHNA / KRISHNA KRISHNA HARE
HARE

3 GOVINDA NAARAAYANA
GOPAALA NAARAAYANA
HARI GOVINDA AANANDA NAARAAYANA

Names of Lord Vishnu
The Divine Aspect of Preservation
Glory to Lord Narayana

4 SHRI KRISHNA GOVINDA HARE MURAARI
HEY NAATHA NAARAAYANA VAASUDEVA

Salutations to Lord Krishna, destroyer of Demon Mura.
Lord Narayana, Son of Vasudeva.

5 NATAWARA LAALA GIRIDHAR GOPALA
JAY JAY NANDANA YASODAA KE BAAL

The King of actors is Krishna, holder of the mountain.
Son of Nanda and Yashoda

6 GOVINDA JAY JAY GOPAALA JAY JAY
RAADHAARAMANA HARI GOVINDA JAY JAY

Victory to Govinda, Victory to Gopala
Who is always with Radha.
Consort of Radha, Glory Glory

BHAJO RAADHE GOVINDA

RAGA - Pilu   TAL - Keherwa

BHAJO RAADHE GOVINDA
BHAJO RAADHE GOVINDA
GOPAALA TERAA PYAARAA NAAM HAI
NANDALALAA TERAA PYAARAA NAAM HAI

1   MORA MUKUTA MATHE TILAKA
GAL BAIJANTI MAALAA, PRABHU
KOYEE KAHAI VASUDEVA KE NANDANA
KOYEE KAHAI NANDALAALAA, PRABHU.....

2   JAL MEN GAJA KO GRAHANE GHERA
JAL MEN CHAKRA CHALAAYAA, PRABHU...
JAB JAB BHEEDA PADI BHAKTANA PARA
NANGE PAON AAYA, PRABHU....

3   ARJUNA KARATA TUMANE HAAKAA
BHAARATA BHAI LADAYI, PRABHU...
BHAKTO KE KHATIRA TUME, PRABHU
ADARAA NANDANAAYE PRABHU

4   DRAUPADI NE JABA TUMHI PUKAARAA
SADI ANA BADHAAYI, PRABHU
NAAM KO LE KARA VISHAABHI PEGAYE
DEKHO MIRA BAYI, PRABHU

5   NARSI KA SAB KAAMA SAWAARE
MUJ KO MATA BISARAYE, PRABHU
JANAMA JANAMA SE NAADABRAHMAANANDA
TERAA HI NAAM PUKARE, PRABHU

MEANING

Sing Radhe Govinda - Radhe Govinda.
Your name Gopala is a loving name.
Your name Nandalala is a loving name.

1   Crowned with peacock feathers,
You haveTilak on your forehead
and a garland ofVaijanti (sacred basil) on your neck.
Some people call you Tulasi,
Vasudevaki Nandana(son of Vasudeva and Devaki).
Soma people call you Nandalala (dear son of Nanda).

2   You saved the elephant who was caught
by alligators in the water by using your chakra (circular sharp missile).
Whenever your devotees were in trouble
you ran barefoot to help them.

3   You drove Arjun's chariot in the big war of Mahabharat.
    For your devotees, O Lord, you came so readily.

4   When Draupadi called you in her trouble
    you came running and made her sari long enough to protect her.
    Just chanting your name Mirabai drank the poison.

5   You have helped Narsi too. Please don't forget me.
    Knowing all this, Brahmanand sings only your name
    and therefore says to everyone: Sing Radhe Govinda.

RAADHE SHYAAM

VIPINAVIHAAREE	RAADHE SHYAAM
KUNJAVIHAAREE	RAADHE SHYAAM
BANKEVIHAREE	RAADHE SHYAAM
DEVAKINANDANA	RAADHE SHYAAM
GOPIKAAVALLABHA	RAADHE SHYAAM
RAADHAAVALLABHA ·	RAADHE SHYAAM
KRISHNAMURAARI	RAADHE SHYAAM
KARUNAASAAGARA	RAADHE SHYAAM
BHAKTIDAAYAKA	RAADHE SHYAAM
MUKTIDAAYAKA	RAADHE SHYAAM
SATCHIDAANANDA	RAADHE SHYAAM
SATGURUROOPA	RAADHE SHYAAM
SARVAROOPA SREE	RAADHE SHYAAM
SARVANAAMA SREE	RAADHE SHYAAM
RAADHE SHYAAM	RAADHE SHYAAM

MEANING

Sporter in the forest - Radhe (Name of Gopi) Shyam (Lord Krishna)
Sporter in bowers - Radhe Shyam
Beautiful sporter - Radhe Shyam
Son of Devaki - Radhe Shyam
Beloved of Gopis - Radhe Shyam
Beloved of Radha - Radhe Shyam
Krishna, the destroyer of Mura (a demon) - Radhe Shyam
Ocean of compassion - Radhe Shyam
Giver of Bhakti (devotion) - Radhe Shyam
Giver of enjoyments - Radhe Shyam
Giver of Mukti - Radhe Shyam
Existence, Knowledge, Bliss - Radhe Shyam
True teacher of all - Radhe Shyam
In all forms - Radhe Shyam
In all names - Radhe Shyam

GOPAALAA

RAGA - Pilu   TAL - Keherwa

1 GOPAALAA GOPAALAA GOKULA NANDANA GOPAALAA
   GOPAALAA GOPAALAA DEVAKI NANDANA GOPAALAA
   NAVANITA CHORA GOPAALAA
   NANDA MUKUNDA GOPAALAA

2 GOPAALAA GOPAALAA VRINDAVANA CHANDRA GOPAALAA
   KAALIYA MARDANA GOPAALAA
   YADU KULA TILAKA GOPAALAA
   GOPAALAA GOPAALAA VRINDAAVANA CHANDRA GOPAALA
   GOPI MANOHARA GOPAALAA
   GOVARDHAN DHARA GOPAALAA

3 GOPAALAA GOPAALAA GOKULA NANDANA GOPAALA
   VENU VINODA GOPAALAA
   YASODA BAALA GOPAALAA
   GOPAALAA GOPAALAA DEVAKI NANDANA GOPAALAA
   MURALI MANOHARA GOPAALAA
   DWAARAKA NAAYAKA GOPAALAA
   GOPAAALA GOPAALAA GOKULA NANDANA GOPAALAA

MEANING

1 Krishna, Krishna, the joy of Gokul.
   Krishna, Krishna, the joy of Devaki.
   Krishna, the stealer of butter, the little son of Nanda.

2 Krishna, the moon of Vrindavan who killed the evil serpent.
   Krishna the jewel among the Yadu Dynasty.
   Krishna the moon of Vrindavan.
   Krishna, the beloved of the cowherd girls.
   The one who held up the Govardhana mountain.

3 Krishna Krishna the joy of Gokul.
   The flute player.
   The son of Yashoda.
   Krishna, Krishna the son of Devaki and Nandana.
   The charming flute player
   The king of Dwaraka.
   Krishna, Krishna, the joy of Gokul.

KRISHNA BHAJANS

KRISHNA MURAARI

RAGA - Dani   TAL - Adital

KRISHNA MANTRA

> OM KLEEM KRISHNAAYA GOVINDAAYA
> GOPEE JANA VALLABHAAYA SWAAHAA

BHAJAN

1. KRISHNA MURAARI BINA TIKARAA TA BALA HARI
   CHURIYA KARATA BANGALI MURAKHA CHATIYA
   DHARATA LAAJA NA AIYEE NITULAKA NAHI TITULAKA
   RATA DHARATA NAAHI MAI TO HARI

2. SABA HI NARANAARI DEKHATA LAAJAATA
   ITA OOTA KAAHE KU MUS KAATA
   EISE JAANE DE ABAKI BAATA
   RAHONGI RAATA SUNONGI BAATA
   CHALONGI SAATHA
   RATIYA AANE DE GHARAKU JAANE DE
   SAASA SUNATA DEGE GAARI

SARGAM

> KRISHNA MURAARI BINA G R S M G R S P M G R S N S G M
> KRISHNA MURAARI BINA S G M P N S N P M G R S N S G M
> KRISHNA MURAARI BINA G M P N S R S N P M P G M G R S
> KRISHNA MURAARI BINA G S M G P M N P S N G R S N P M

MEANING

1. O Lord Krishna you are breaking my bangles,
   you are twisting my wrist and holding my breast
   and yet you are not feeling ashamed.
   You are not fearing anyone and I am defeated.

2. All men and women are looking and I am feeling shy.
   You are smiling, looking this side and that side.
   Let me go this time. I will stay some other time in the night.
   I will hear your talk and stories, and I will walk with you.
   Night is approaching now let me go home.
   If my mother in law hears she will abuse me.

ADHARAM MADHURAM (Sri Vallabhacharyakritam)

RAGA - Shivaranjani   TAL - Keherwa

SHLOKA

SHAANTAAKAARAM BHUJAGASHAYANAM
PADMANAABHAM SURESHAM
VISHVAADHAARAM GAGANASADRISHAM
MEGHAVARNAM SHUBHAANGAM
LAKSHMEEKAANTAM KAMALANAYANAM
YOGIBHIRDHYAANAGAMYAM
VANDE VISHNUM BHAVABHAYAHARAM
SARVALOKAIKA NATHAM

MEANING

I bow to that Lord Vishnu, whose form is Peace,
who is sleeping on the bed of snake (Adisesha),
who has Lotus in the navel, who is Lord of Gods,
who is the support of this world, who is like ether,
whose color is like cloud, whose limbs are beautiful,
who is the consort of the Goddess Lakshi whose eyes are like lotus,
who is attainable by Yogins through meditation,
who destroys fear of Samsara and who is the one Lord of all the worlds.

ADHARAM MADHURAM

1   ADHARAM MADHURAM VADANAM MADHURAM
    NAYANAM MADHURAM HASITAM MADHURAM
    HRIDAYAM MADHURAM GAMANAM MADHURAM
    MADHURAA DHIPATERAKHILAM MADHURAM

2   VACHANAM MADHURAM CHARITAM MADHURAM
    VASANAM MADHURAM VALITAM MADHURAM
    CHALITAM MADHURAM BHRAMITAM MADHURAM
    MADHURAA DHIPATE......

3   VENUR MADHURO RENUR MADHURO
    PANIR MADHURAH PADAU MADHURAU
    NRITYAM MADHURAM SAKHYAM MADHURAM
    MADHURAA DHIPATE.....

4   GEETAM MADHURAM PEETAM MADHURAM
    MUKTAM MADHURAM SUPTAM MADHURAM
    ROOPAM MADHURAM TILAKAM MADHURAM
    MADHURAA DHIPATE.....

5   KARANAM MADHURAM TARANAM MADHURAM
    HARANAM MADHURAM RAMANAM MADHURAM
    VAMITAM MADHURAM SHAMITAM MADHURAM
    MADHURAA DHIPATE......

6   GUNJAA MADHURAA MAALAA MADHURAA
     YAMUNA MADHURAA VICHI MADHURAA
     SALILAM MADHURAM KAMALAM MADHURAM
     MADHURAA DHIPATE....

7   GOPEE MADHURAA LILAA MADHURAA
     YUKTAM MADHURAM MUKTAM MADHURAM
     DRISHTAM MADHURAM SHISHTAM MADHURAM
     MADHURAA DHIPATE....

8   GOPAA MADHURAA GAVO MADHURAA
     YASHTIR MADHURAA SRISHTIR MADHURAA
     DALITAM MADHURAM PHALITAM MADHURAM
     MADHURAA DHIPATE..

MEANING

1   Sweet are the lips, the face, the eyes and the smile;
     sweet are the heart, the gait -
     everything of the Lord of Madhura is sweet.

2   Sweet are the words, the conduct, the clothes and the impulses;
     sweet are the movements, the walks -
     everything of the Lord of Madhura is sweet.

3   Sweet is the flute, the dust (of his feet), the hands and the feet;
     sweet are the dances, the friendship -
     everything of the Lord of Madhura is sweet.

4   Sweet are the songs, the drinks, the release, the sleep;
     sweet are the form, the sacred mark on the forehead -
     everything of the Lord Of Madhura is sweet.

5   Sweet are the actions, the crossing over, the enchantment, the dalliance;
     sweet are the emanations, the communion -
     everything of the Lord of Madhura is sweet.

6   Sweet are the "Gunjas" (a small red black berry with which boy Krishna
     was fond of playing), the garlands, the river Yamuna and the wavelets
     therein; sweet is the water of Yamuna, the lotus -
     everything of the Lord of Madhura is sweet.

7   Sweet are the milkmaids (Gopis), the sports (Lila), the union and separation;
     sweet is the vision, the remnants (That is left after the Lord's enjoyment)
     everything of the Lord of Madhura is sweet.

8   Sweet are the Gopas (cowherds), the cows,
     the staff (used by the cowherds) and creation;
     sweet is destruction, production of result
     everything of the Lord of Madhura is sweet.

AB KE TEK HAMAAREE

RAGA - Pilu   TAL - Tintal

AB KE TEK HAMAAREE MURAREE
AB KE TEK HAMAAREE
LAAJ RAAKHO GIRIDHAAREE
AB KE TEK HAMAAREE

1   JAISEE LAAJ RAAKHEE ARJUN KEE
BHAARAT YUDHA MOJAREE
SARATHEE BANKAR RATHA KO HAA KYO
CHAKRA SUDARSHAN DHAREE
BHAGAT KEE TEKA NA TALEE
ABA KE TEK HAMAAREE MURAREE

2   JAISEE LAAJ RAAKHEE DRAUPADI KEE
HONE NADEE NE UGHAREE
KHECHAT DO BHUJ THAAKE
DUSHAASAN PATHE HAREE
CHEER BARHAYO MURAAREE
ABA KE TEK HAMAAREE MURAAREE

3   SURDAS KEE LAAJA RAAKHO
AB KO HAI RAKHAVAAREE
SHREE VAR SHREE VAR RAADHAA PYAAREE
SHREE BRISHBHANU DULAAREE
SHARANA TOREE AAYO MURAAREE
ABA KE TEK HAMAAREE MURAAREE
LAAJ RAAKHO GIRIDHAAREE

MEANING

(The Devotee is pleading with Krishna that
if you do not appear to me, people will laugh at me.
I will get a bad reputation.)

1   This time oh my Krishna, save me Giridhar.
As you saved Arjuna in war.
In the Mahabharat war you became his charioteer.
You held Sudarshan Chakra.
You did not reject the vow of your devotee.
So this time again Oh My Krishna
please give me your darshan.

2   As you saved Draupadi
when Dushashan started pulling out her sari
with his two strong hands,
you went running there with your magic spell
and gave a continuous supply of saris

until Dushashan got tired.
The same way this time you come to me Krishna.
Save me from a bad reputation.

3   Save Surdas and give your darshan.
Who is there other than you to protect me.
I surrender to you completely.
Please accept me as your dear Radha.
But this time please give me your darshan.
Come to me. Save me Oh my Krishna.

BHAJAN

KAISE KAISE JAHON (See Bhajan 1 Pg.80)

MURALI GAANASUDHAA

RAGA - Darbari Kanada   Tal - Keherwa

SHLOKA

ADAU DEVAKEEDEVGARBHAJANANAM
GOPIGRIHE VARDHANAM
MAAYAA POOTANAJIVITAPAHARANAM
GOVARDHANODDHAARANAM
KAMSACHHEDANA KAURAVADIHANANAM
KUNTEESUTAAPAALANAM
ETAT BHAAGAVATAM PURAANAKATHITAM
SRI KRISHNALEELAMRITAM

MEANING

Beginning with birth in Devaki Devi's womb
and then growing up in the house of the Gopi
(cowherd-woman - Yasoda),
killing of crafty Putana,
holding up of the Mount Govardhana,
destruction of Kamsa and others,
annihilation of Kauravas and their partisans,
protecting of the sons of Kunti
these in short are the nectar like Leelas of Sri Krishna
contained in the epic of Bhagavata.

BHAJAN

MURALI GAANA SUDHAA KUNJABIHAREE
VRINDAAVANA SANCHAAREE SHREE HARI

1 MRIGADHAR GIRIDHARA MUKUNDA MAADHAVA
SURANARAVANDITA SHUBU VARA DATA
RAADHAA VALLABHA RAMANEE MANOHARA
VAASUDEVA HARA SHRI JAGANAATHA
MURALEE GANASUDHA KUNJA BIHAREE
VRINDA VANA SANCHAARI SHREE HARI

2 INDIRAA RAMANA SHREE HARI VITHALA
KRISHNA YADUKULA NANDKISHORA
PEETAM BARADHARA PATITA GOPAALA
VAANI VIRACHITA GEETA GOPAALA
MURALI GAANA SUDHAA KUNJA BIHAREE
VRINDAAVANA SANCHAREE SHREE HARI

MEANING

The flute player Krishna sports in the beautiful garden of the Gods.
He who lives in Vrindavan.

1 The peacock feathered, savior of Giridhar Mountain, Krishna.
Devas and humans offer their salutations to the giver of happiness.
The beauty of Radha's Beloved Krishna attracts all the women.
Vasudeva's son, the protector of the world.Beautiful Shri Krishna.

2 Nanda's son Krishna is born in the Yadukula dynasty.
He who wearsyellow silk robe is the saviour of the sinful.
I am singing this poem of Gopala, the flute player Krishna
who pervades every where, in the beautiful garden of God
that is this Earth.

GOPAALA GOKULA

RAGA - Yaman Kalyan   TAL - Rupak

SHLOKA

1   VASUDEVASUTAM DEVAM
    KAMSA CHANOORAMARDANAM
    DEVAKEEPARAMAANANDAM
    KRISHNAM VANDE JAGADGURUM

2   KRISHNAAYA VAASUDEVAAYA
    HARAYE PARMAATMANE
    PRAANATAH KLESHANAA SHAAYA
    GOVINDAAYA NAMONAMAH

3   KARAARAVINDE NAPADARAVINDAM
    MUKHAARAVINDE VINIVESHAYANTAM
    VATASYA PATRASYA PUTE SHAYAANAM
    BALAM MUKUNDAM MANASAA SMAARAMI

MEANING

1   I bow to the world teacher, Lord Krishna,
    Who is the son of Vasudeva,
    Who killed Kamsa and Chanoora and
    Who is the Supreme Bliss of Devaki.

2   Lord Krishna, Who is Vasudevas soul,
    Who is the Supreme Soul
    who destroys all evil and all difficulties,
    Salutations to that Lord Krishna
    who protects the cows.

3   He picks up his lotus like foot with his lotus like hand
    and keeps it near his lotus like mouth
    as he lies on the leaf of a tree.
    That young Lord Krishna I worship in my mind.

BHAJAN

1 GOPAALA GOKULA BALLABHIPRIYA
   GOPAA GOSUTA BALLABHAM
   CHARANAARAVINDAM AHAM BHAJE
   BHAJANIYA SURAMUNI DURLABHAM

2 GHANA SHYAAMA KAAMA ANEKACCHAVI
   LOKAABHIRAAMA MANOHARAM
   KINJALKA VASANA KISHORAMOORATI
   BHOORI GUNA KARUNAAKARAM

3 SHIRA KEKIPINCCHA VILOLA KUNDALA
   ARUNA BANARUHALOCHANAM
   GUNGAVATAMSA VICHITRA SABANGA
   DHATU BHAVABHAYA MOCHANAM

4 KACHA KUTILA SUNDARA TILAKA BHROO
   RAAKAA MAYANKA SAMAANANAM
   APAAHARANA TULASIDASA TRAASA
   VIHAARA VRINDA KAANANAM

MEANING

O Gopala (cowherd), Beloved of the damsels of Gokula,
Lord of the cowherds, cows and calves, O the worshipful,
I worship Thy lotus feet,
which even Devas and Rishis find difficult of attainment.

1 O Thou of the darkish blue hue like the thickly laden clouds,
   Who hath the splendour of countless Cupids,
   Who delighteth the worlds,
   Who art so beautiful as to attract the minds of all,
   Who weareth yellow silken cloth, Who art in the form of a little boy,
   Who art very compassionate. (I worship Thy Lotus feet).

2 O Thou Whose head is adorned by the peacock's feather,
   Who hath vibrating earrings, Whose eyes are like the red lotus,
   Who wears flower garlands on head, Whose limbs are very graceful and
   Who liberateth (the devotees) from the fear of birth and death
   (I worship Thy lotus feet).

3 O Thou Who hath curly hairs, beautiful Tilak
   (mark on the forehead between the eye-brows)
   and charming eye-brows and a face equal to the Full Moon,
   Who destroyeth the fears of Tulasidasa and
   Who sporteth in the forests of Vrindavan (I worship Thy Lotus feet).

AAJ NANDALAALA SAKHEE

RAGA - Bhairav   TAL - Jhaptal

AAJA NANDALAALA SAKHEE
PREMA MARDA KAPI
SANGA LA LA NAARIYE
JAMUNAA TIYA RE BHARAANA

PHOOLI KE SARAKA MAALAA
MAALATI SAGHANA BANA
MANDA SUGHANDA SHEETALA
SAMEERE BHARANA

MEGHA CHAMPAKA BHHARANA
KRISHNA RASA MAATEI
RAAGA PANCHAMA SUHE
KUTILA HALAKAANA

EKA MUKHA JORA SAKHEE
DHARA RAHE DHYAANA SABA
AAPA NOW LAALA CHITTA
CHURA PAYEE BHARANA

SARGAM

AAJA NANDA	P M G R G R S / D P M P G M P M G R S R
AAJA NANDA	N R G R G R S / N R G M P M G R G R S R
AAJA NANDA	P M P G M P / D P M P G M P M G R S R
AAJA NANDA	R S G R M G P M D P N D S N D P M G R S
AAJA NANDA	S R G R/ R G M G/ G M P M/ M P D P M G R
S	
AAJA NANDA	S R G M P D N S / S R G R S N D P M G R S

MEANING

Oh my friends, today Lord Krishna is coming.
We are all so happy to know that we will be
playing with him on the banks of the Yamuna.
All of nature is happy,
the flowers are giving its light fragrance,
a cool breeze is blowing,
the clouds are dancing.

Everyone and everything are full of the bliss of Krishna.
Meditating, singing and giving salutations
to the one that steals the mind and heart.

BANAVAAREE BANE

RAGA - Bhairav   TAL - Tintal

    BANAVAREE BANE MURARE HA
    KUNJA BIHAREE
    GIRIDHAR SANGA SOHE RAADHAA PYAREE
    BRIJA BANKE DULAREE
    BANAVAREE BANE

    BANAVAREE BANE
    P M G R G M P D N D P M G R S

    VAREE BANE
    S R G M P D N S / S N D P M G R S

    VAREE BANE
    S N D N S R G R S N D P M G R S

    VAREE BANE

    TEERA TILAKANA PYAREE
    NAASEEKAAMUTI SA WARI
    MURALI ADHAR SAPTA SOORA NA BISAREE
    BANAVAREE BANE MURARE HA BANA

MEANING

    The one who plays in the garden is Krishna.
    He looks beautiful in the company of Radha.
    Radha is the favorite of Krishna.
    When he plays the flute it is never out of tune.

SHLOKA - SHANTAKARAM

Raga - Bhairav

SHAANTAAKAARAM BHUJAGASHAYANAM
PADMANAABHAM SURESHAM
VISHVAADHAARAM GAGANASADRISHAM
MEGHAVARNAM SHUBHAANGAM
LAKSHMEEKAANTAM KAMALANAYANAM
YOGIBHIRDHYAANAGAMYAM
VANDE VISHNUM BHAVABHAYAHARAM
SARVALOKAIKA NATHAM

MEANING

I bow to that Lord Vishnu, whose form is Peace,
who is sleeping on the bed of snake (Adisesha),
who has Lotus in the navel, who is Lord of Gods,
who is the support of this world, who is like ether,
whose color is like cloud, whose limbs are beautiful,
who is the consort of the Goddess Lakshmi,
whose eyes are like lotus,
who is attainable by Yogins through meditation,
who destroys fear of Samsara and
who is the one Lord of all the worlds.

HARI OM NAMO NARAAYANAYA (Mantra)

Raga - Bhairav   Tal - Keherwa

Narayana is another name of Lord Vishnu who is the preserver. After creation, it is the energy of Lord Vishnu that puts order to the universe. Whenever this balance is disturbed it is Lord Vishnu that incarnates from time to time in whatever form is necessary to restore balance. Whenever righteousness and goodness are overshadowed by evil forces, Lord Narayana incarnates to destroy the sin of the sinner and to restore Dharma.
This Mantra ," Om Namo Narayanaya", is very effective in bringing about peace, harmony and balance in one's physical, mental and spiritual life and should be chanted for world peace.

NARAAYANA KA NAMA NIRALA

RAGA - Desh   TAL - Keherwa

(See Bhajan 1 Pg. 76)

NARAAYANA SHRIMAN NARAAYAN

RAGA - Kedar   TAL - Tintal

```
S N R S / R P / M P D P M G P / S N R S / R P /
M P D N S N D P / M P D N D P / M P D P M G P / S N R S
```

1   NARAAYANA SHRIMAN NARAAYANA
    KAMALAA PATI JAGA KE RAKHAWAAREE
    CHARANO ME LOTATA KAMALAA DAASI
    NAABHI KAMALAA ME BRAHMA VIRAAJE

2   KSHIRA SINDHUME SESHA NAGAPARA
    CHARANA PADATA HAY INDRITI HARI
    UTTA PATTI STITI LAYAKE KARATAA
    SAKALA SHRISTI SAMPARA NAKARAYEE

3   BHUMI BARA UTARANA KARANA
    TUMA HILIYO MANUJA AVATAARE
    MAHIMAA TUMHARE APARAMPAARE
    PAPI JANAKE TAARANA HARE

MEANING

1   Salutations to Lord Narayana, the world protecter.
    Lakshmi, his consort, sits devotedly at his feet.
    From his navel sprung the Lotus
     from which Lord Brahma emerged.

2   Lord Vishnu reclines on the Serpent "Shesha Naga"
    that floats on the ocean of milk.
    Lord, you are the creator, preserver and destroyer.
    Indra and all the other Gods bow down to your feet.

3   You are the cause of the removal of the world's burdens.
    You have taken a human form as an Avatar.
    Your glory is beyond description.
    You are the redeemer of the sinful.

CHANT

NARAAYANA NARAAYANA JAI GOVINDA HARE
NARAAYANA NARAAYANA JAI GOPALA HARE

RAAMA KRISHNA GOVINDA NARAAYANA

RAGA - Bhairavi   TAL - Keherwa

RAAMA KRISHNA GOVINDA NARAAYANA
SHRI NIVASA GOVINDA NARAAYANA
RADHA KRISHNA GOVINDA NARAAYANA
PANDURANGA GOVINDA NARAAYANA
JAYA HARI GOVINDA NARAAYANA

RAAMA KRISHNA GOVINDA NARAAYANA
SITA PATI GOVINDA NARAAYANA
RAAMA KRISHNA GOVINDA NARAAYANA
BHAJA MANA NARAAYANA
LAKSHMI NARAAYANA
HARI NARAAYANA
OM NARAAYANA
HARI NARAAYANA
LAKSHMI NARAAYANA
BHAJA MANA NARAAYANA
OM NARAAYANA

CHANT

SHRI MAN NARAAYANA

SHRI MAN NARAAYANA NARAAYANA NAARAYANA
BHAJA MAN NARAYANA NARAAYANA NARAAYANA

HARI NARAAYANA NARAAYANA NARAAYANA
LAKSHMI NARAAYANA NARAAYANA NARAAYANA

BADRI NARAAYANA NARAAYANA NARAAYANA
SURYA NARAAYANA NARAAYANA NARAAYANA

SITA RAMA KAHO RADHE SHYAMA KAHO

NIRVAANA SHATKAM

Raga: Yaman Kalyan   Tala: Dipchandi

1 MANO BUDDHYA AHAMKARA / CHITAANI NAHAM
   NA CHA SHROTRA JIH WAY / NA CHA GHRA NA NETRE
   NA CHAVYOMA BHOOMIR / NA TEJO NA VAYUR
   CHIDAANANDA ROOPAHA / SHIVOHAM SHIVOHAM

2 NA CHA PRAANA SAMJNO / NA VAI PANCHAVAAYUR
   NA VAA SAPTA DHAATUR / NA VAA PANCHA KOSHAHA
   NA VAAK PAANI PADAU / NA CHOPASTHA PAYOO
   CHIDAANANDA.......

3 NA ME DWESHA RAAGAU / NA ME LOBHA MOHAU
   MADO NAIVA ME NAIVA / MAATSARYA BHAAVAHA
   NA DHARMO NA CHAARTHO / NA KAAMO NA MOKSHAH
   CHIDAANANDA......

4 NA PUNYAM NA PAAPAM / NA SAUKHYAM NA DUHKHAM
   NA MANTRO NA TEERTHAM / NA VEDA NA YAGNAH
   AHAM BHOJANAM NAIVA / BHOYAM NA BHOKTAAH
   CHIDAANANDA.....

5 NA ME MRITYU SHANKAA / NA ME JATIBHEDAHA
   PITA ANAIVA ME NAIVA / MAATAA NA JANMAH
   NA BANDHUR NA MITRAM / GURURNAIVA SHISHYAH
   CHIDAANANDA.....

6 AHAM NIRVIKALPO / NIRAA KARA ROOPAH
   VIBHOTWAM CHASARVATRA / SARVE INDRIYANA
   SADA ME SAMAATWAM / NA MUKTIR NA BANDAH
   CHIDAANANDA......

MEANING

1   Neither am I the mind, nor the intellect nor egoism , nor mindstuff; Neither am I the senses of hearing, taste, smell or sight; Neither am I the ether, the earth, the light, the wind; I am Existence Absolute, Knowledge Absolute, Bliss Absolute; I am Siva I am Siva.

2   Neither am I the vital force Prana nor the five vital airs; Neither am I water, the seven elements of body nor the five sheaths; Neither am I the organs of action, nor object of senses; I am Existence Absolute, Knowledge Absolute; Bliss Absolute; I am Siva I am Siva.

3   Neither have I love nor hatred, neither greed nor infatuation; Neither egotism, nor envy, neither Dharma (duty in the form of Shastric injunctions) nor longing for Moksha; Neither am I desire, nor objects of desire, I am Existence , Knowledge and Bliss Absolute; I am Siva

4   Neither have I virtue nor sin, neither happiness nor misery; Nor Mantras nor pilgrimages, nor scriptures nor sacrifices; Neither the object of enjoying, nor act of enjoyment nor enjoyer; I am Existence Absolute, Knowledge Absolute, Bliss Absolute; I am Siva I am Siva.

5   Neither have I fear of death nor caste distinction; Neither have I birth, nor have I parents, friends and relatives; Neither have I guru nor disciple; I am Existence Absolute, Knowledge Absolute, Bliss Abso-lute; I am Siva I am Siva.

6   Neither am I touched by senses nor subject to change; I am without form, I pervade everywhere; I am ever the same, I have neither liberation nor bondage; I am Existence Absolute, Knowledge Abso-lute, Bliss Absolute; I am Siva I am Siva.

BADRINATH VISHWAMBHARAM

RAGA - Yaman Kalyan   TAL - Rupak

SHLOKA

SHAANTAAKAARAM BHUJAGASHAYANAM
PADMANAABHAM SURESHAM
VISHVAADHAARAM GAGANASADRISHAM
MEGHAVARNAM SHUBHAANGAM
LAKSHMEEKAANTAM KAMALANAYANAM
YOGIBHIRDHYAANAGAMYAM
VANDE VISHNUM BHAVABHAYAHARAM
SARVALOKAIKA NATHAM

BADRINATH VISHWAMBHARAM

RAGA - Yaman Kalyan   TAL - Rupa

1. PAVANA MANDA SUGANDHA SHEETALA
   HEMA MANDIR SHOBHITAM
   NIKATA GANGAA BAHATA NIRMALA
   BADRINAATH VISHWAMBHARAM
   SHREE BADRINAATH.....

2. SHESHA SUMIRANA KARATA NISHADIN
   DHARATA DHYAANA MAHESHWARAM
   SHREE VEDA BRAHMA KARATA STUTI
   SHREE BADRINAATH ......

3. INDRA CHANDRA KUBER DINKARA
   DHOOPA DEEPA PRAKAASHITAM
   SIDDHA MUNIJANA KARATA JAY JAY
   BADRINAATH........

4. SHAKTI GAURI GANESH SHAARADAA
   NAARADA MUNI UCHARAARANAM
   YOGEE DHYAANA APAARA LEELA
   BADRINAATH....

5. YAKSHA KINNARA KARATA KAUTOOKA
   TAALA VEENA VEDITAM
   SHREE LAKSHMI KAMALA CHAMARA DHOLE
   BADRINAATH....

6. HIMA PATHA KEDAAR DARSHANA
   SIDDHA MUNIJANA SEVITAM
   HIMAALAYA MEN SUKHA SWAROOPA
   BADRINAATH....

7. TAPTA KUND KE ADHIKA MAHIMAA
   DASHADI SHAANANA SHOBHITAM
   NARANARAAYANA KARATA STUTI SHREE
   BADRINAATH....

8. SHREE BADRINAATH KE SAPTRARATRA
   PARAMA PAAPA VI NAA SHANAM
   KOTI TIRTH SWAROOPA PURAANA
   BADRINAATH....

MEANING

1. A cool fragrant wind is blowing.
   The temple is decorated with snow.
   Near the temple the Ganges is flowing quietly.
   Badrinath is the sustainer of the world.

2. Sheshnaag is meditating every day and night on Badrinath.
   Veda and Brahma are doing prayers to Badrinath,
   with kindling incense andlamp.

3. Indra, Chandra, Kubira, the sun,
   Munis and Rishis are daily uttering Victory to Badrinath.
   They are all shining with their own light.
   The realized Munis are praying.

4. Shakti, Gauri, Ganesha, Sharada and
   Narada are every day chanting Lord Badrinaths name.
   Yogis and Saints are doing meditation on
   the limitless divine plays of the Lord.

5. Yakshas, Kinaras play music on the vina and drums.
   The wife of Vishnu, Lakshmi is fanning herself.

6. In Kedar Temple, on Himalayas, near to Badrinath,
   the way of snow, Siddhas are doing daily worship, full of bliss.

7. Hot spring water comes from a small well.
   If you have Darshan here you can cure disease.
   Man and Gods are praying to Badrinath.

8. Badrinath is sitting on a chariot of seven horses
   (Badrinath is on top of all the mountains).
   One pilgrimage to Badrinath is equal to thousands of
   Scriptures and pilgrimages together, and it destroysall sins.

ACHYUTAM KESAVAM
(Sri Sankaracharyakritam)

RAGA - Bheempalas   TAL - Dadra

SHLOKA

> YAM BRAHMAA VARUNENDRARUDRAMARUTAH
> STUNWANTI DIVYAIH STAVAIH
> VEDAIH SAANGAPADAKRAMOPANISHADAIH
> GAAYANTI YAM SAAMAGAAH
> DHYAANAAVASTHITATAADGATENA MANASAA
> PASHYANTI YAM YOGINO
> YASYANTAM NA VIDUH SURAASURAGANAA
> DEVAAYA TASMAI NAMAH

MEANING

> Salutations to that god whom Brahma,
> Indra, Varuna, Rudra and the Maruts
> praise with Divine Hymns.
> Of Whom the Sama chanters
> sing by the Vedas and their Angas,
> (in the Pada and Krama methods),
> and by the Upanishads.
> Whom the Yogis see with their minds
> absorbed in Him through meditation
> and Whose ends the hosts of Devas
> and Asuras know not.

(Eight Verses On Lord Vishnu)

1 ACHYUTAM KESHAVAM RAAMANAARAYAANAM
   KRISHNADAAMODARAM VAASUDEVAM HARIM
   SREEDHARAM MADHAVAM GOPIKAAVALLABHAM
   JAANAKEENAAYAKAM RAAMACHANDRAM BHAJE

2 ACHYUTAM KESHAVAM SATYABHAAMAADHAVAM
   MAADHAVAM SREEDHARAM RAADHIKAARADHITAM
   INDIRAAMANDIRAM CHETASAA SUNDARAM
   DEVAKEENANDANAM NANDAJAM SANDAJHE

3 VISHNAVE JISHNAVE SANKHINE CHAKRINE
   RUKMINEERAGEENE JAANAKEEJANAYE
   VALLAVEEVALLABHAYAARCHITAYAATMANE
   KAMSAVIDHVANSINE VANSINE TE NAMAH

4 KRISHNA GOVINDA HE RAAMA NAARAAYANA
   SRIPATE VASUDEVAJITA SRINIDHE
   ACHYUTAANANDA HE MAADHAVAADHOKSHAJA
   DVAARAKANAAYAKA DRAUPADEERAKSHAKA

5 RAKSHASAKSHOBHITAH SITAYA SHOBHITO
   DANDAKAARANYABHUPUNYATAKAARANA
   LAKSHMANENANVITO VANARAISSEVITO
   AGASTYASAMPOOJITO RAAGHAVAH PAATU MAAM

6 DHENUKARISHTAKANISHTAKRIDVESHITAH
   KESIHA KAMSAHRIDVAMSHIKAAVAADAKA
   PUTANAKOPAKAH SURAJAKHELANO
   BAALAGOPAALAKAH PAATU MAAM SARVADAA

7 VIDYUDUDYOTAVAT PRASPHURADVASASAM
   PRAVRIDAMBHODAVAT PROLLASADVIGRAHAM
   VANYAYA MALAYA SHOBHITORAHSTHALAM
   LOHITANGHRIDWAYAM VARIJAKSHAM BHAJE

8 KUNCHITAIH KUNTALAIRBHRAJAMANANANAM
   RATNAMAULIM LASATKUNDALAM GANDAYOH
   HARAKEYURAKAM KANKANAPROJVALAM
   KINKINEEMANJULAM SYAMALAM TAM BHAJE

9 ACHYUTASYASHTAKAM YAH PATHEDISHTADAM
   PREMATAH PRATYAHAM PURUSHAH SASPRIHAM
   VRITTATAH SUNDARAM KARTRU VISHVAMBHARAH
   TASYA VASHYO HARIRJAYATE SATVARAM

MEANING

1   I worship Achyuta (Invincible), Keshava, Rama, Narayana,
    Krishna, Damodara, Vasudeva, Hari,
    Sridhara, Madhava, the beloved of Gopis,
    the Lord of Sita, Sri Ramachandra.

2   I meditate upon Achyuta, Keshava, the Lord of Satyabhama,
    the Lord of Lakshmi, Sridhara, adored by Sri Radha,
    the abode of Lakshmi, most beautiful,
    the son of Devaki, the son of Nanda.

3   I salute Thee, who art all pervading, victorious,
    bearer of conch and discus, beloved of Rukmini, consort of Janaki (Sita),
    the very life of the Gopis, supremely adorable,
    my own Self, destroyer of Kamsa, bearer of flute.

4   O Krishna, O Govinda, O Rama, O Narayana,
    O Lord of Lakshmi, O Vasudeva, O unconquerable One,
    O abode of beauty, O Achyuta, O Ananta (Infinite One),
    O Madhava (destroyer of demon Madhu), O Adhokshaja (beyond senses),
    O Lord of Dwaraka, O Protector of Draupadi - be gracious to me.

5   May Sri Ramachandra, born in Raghu dynasty, wrathful towards demons,
    shining in the company of Sita who made the Dandaka forest auspicious,
    who is followed by Lakshmana, who is served by mon-keys,
    and who is adored by the sage Agastya - protect me.

6   May He ever protect me who destroyed the demons Dhenuka and Arish-
    ta,
    who is the destroyer of enemies, the slayer of Keshi and Kamsa,
    who plays on the flute, who is angered against Putana,
    who sports on the banks of the Yamuna River.

7   I worship that lotus eyed Hari whose yellow silk cloth shines like lighten-
    ing,
    whose body is as swarthy as the clouds laden with rain,
    whose chest is adorned with the garlands of forest flowers
    and whose feet are of red colour.

8   I worship Shyam Sundara (blue complexioned and beautiful one)
    whose forehead is adorned by curly locks, and the head with jewelled
    crown,
    whose cheeks shine by the brilliance of beautiful earrings,
    who is adorned with garland, armlets and bracelets.

9   One who daily chants these eight verses about Achyuta
    composed in beautiful rhymes which are bestowers of desires,
    he verily wins Lord Hari,
    the Creator of the whole universe.

PHASA GAIYA

RAGA - Bheempalas   TAL - Jaleka

1   PHASA GAIYA DUNIYA TAMAAMA
    PHASA GAIYA DUNIYA TAMAAMA
    BISU TI NARA TANUWA KAMA
    KAAMA KRODHA SAHE BRAHMARA
    PHASA GAIYA DUNIYA TAMAAMA

2   KO KOHI NAHI JAAGRATA
    TAKE SU MRITYU KALI
    KO KATA NAHI NIRUTA KAMA
    KAAMA KRODHA SAHE BRAHMARA
    PHASA GAIYA DUNIYA TAMAAMA

MEANING

1   We are trapped in this world play.
    The whole world is entrapped in the cycle of action.
    Men are living just for the body.
    They are suffering from lust and anger -
    like a honey bee in the lotus,
    the whole world is trapped.

2   No one is awakened.
    Death is waiting yet no one stops working.
    They are suffering from lust and anger,
    like a honeybee they are entrapped
    in the world of action.

GORA MUKHAA

RAGA - Bheempalas   TAL - Tintal

1   GORA MUKHAA SU MORE MANA BHAAVE
    LAKA CHUPA DARASHANA ATAHI SUWAVE
    GORA MUKHA SU MORE MANA BHAVE

2   NAYANA MI RANGA SAMA CHANDRA MUKHI HA
    BADANA KAMALA ATI SURADASA KI
    CHO DAAVE; GORA MUKHA SU MORE MANA BHAVE

MEANING

1   I love very much to see the white handsome face of my Lord.

2   Suradas says that He has black colored eyes,
    moon like face and lotus like body.
    Such a beautiful white faced Lord is preferred by my mind.

NARAAYANA KO

    NAARAAYANA KO BHAJANA KARO NARA
    MUKTI NA HO BINAA BHAJANA TUMHAREE
    NAARAAYANA KO BHAJANA KARO NARA

1. KYA KASHI JAVE / KYA MATHURA JAVE
    KYA KAASHI JAVE P M P G M PN D P M P G M P M P
    KYA KAASHI JAVE / KYA MATHURA JAVE
    KYA KEDAAR JAVE / KYA BADAREE JAVE
    KYA PARAVATA BANA PHIRATA ANAREE
    MUKTI NA HO BINAA BHAJANA TUMHAREE

2. JAPA TAPA YOGA KATHINA KALI MAYI
    SHASTRA ANEKA PADO DINA RATI / MUKTI NA......

3. BHAI BANDHU AURA KUTUMBA PARUWAARA
    KISAKI HO TUMA KAUNA TIHAARA
    SABA APA APANA MATALABA WALA
    KAHATA KABIR SUNNO BHAI SADHO
    AAPA GAYE PICHE DOOBAGAYI DUNIYA / MUKTI NA....

MANA LAAGO

RAGA - Bheempalas   TAL - Keherwa

1 MANA LAAGO MERO YAARA FAKIRI MEN
    JO SUKHA PAVO RAAMA BHAJANA MEN
    SO SUKHA NAAHI AMIRI MEN
    MANA LAAGO MERO YAARA FAKIRI MEN
    JO SUKHA PAVO RAAMA BHAJANA MEN

2 BHALAA BURAA SABA KA SUNA LIJE
    KARA GUJARAAN TU GARIBI MEN
    PREMA NAGARI ME RAHANI HAMAARI
    BHALI BANI AYI SABURI MEN
    MANA LAAGO MERO YAARA FAKIRI MEN
    JO SUKHA PAVO RAAMA BHAJANA MEN

3 HAATHA ME KUNDI BAGALA MEN SOTA
    CHAARON DISI JAAGIRI MEN
    YAHA TANA KHAAKA MILEGA
    KAHAA PHIRATA TU MAGARURI MEN
    MANA LAAGO MERO YAARA FAKIRI MEN
    JO SUKHA PAVO RAAMA BHAJANA MEN

4 KAHATA KABIRAA SUNNO BHAI SADHO
    SAHIBA MILAI SABURI MEN
    MANA LAAGO MERO YAARA FAKIRI MEN
    JO SUKHA PAVO RAAMA BHAJANA MEN

MEANING

1 My mind is inclined to be mendicant. (in complete renunciation).
   The happiness which I get in chanting the name of Rama,
   is not gained in richness.

2 I maintain myself in poverty.
   My residence is in the city of love,
   so I should remain patient to whatever good or evil comes to me.

3 I have a stick in my hand and
   my estate is spread in all the four directions.

4 At the end this body will turn into ashes,
   so why should we live arrogantly?

5 Kabir says, O good brother! Hear me.
   God can be realizedif we have patience.

MAN TARPAT

RAGA - Malkouns   TAL - Tintal

1 MAN TARPAT HARI DARSHAN KO AAJ
   TUMA BINA BIGARE SAGARE KAAJ MANA
   BINATEE KARAT HUN RAKHIYO LAAJ MEREE

2 TUM HARI DWARKA MAI HUN JOGEE
   HAMAREE OUR NAJAR KABA HOGEE
   SUNO MOREE VYAKULA MAN KO AAJ MEREE
   MAN TARPAT HARI DARSHAN KO AAJ

3 BINA GURU JYNANA KAHAAN SE PAVOON
   DEEJO JYNAN TOO HARI GUNA GAVOON
   SAB MUNI JANA PAR TUMHARAA RAAJ MEREE
   MAN TARPAT HARI DARSHAN KO AAJ

MEANING

1 O Lord Sri Krishna, today my heart is aching
   and crying for your divine vision.
   I request that you keep my prestige as a devotee.

2 I am a beggar at your door,
   when will you look towards me?
   Please hear me and see my agitated mind today.

3 Where from shall I have divine knowledge
   except through a Guru.
   Please give me such knowledge
   so that I can sing the glories of Hari.

DIN NEEKE BEETE

RAGA - Malkouns   TAL - Tintal

1   DIN NEEKE BEETE JAATE HAI
    JINA SUMIRANA KARA MANA RAAM NAAM JINA
    TAJA SAKALA JAGATKE VISHA YA KAAM
    JO BOTE HAI SO PATE HAI
    TERE SANGA CHALE NA EK DAAM

2   BHAI BANDHU OUR KUTUMBA PARIWAARA
    KISKE HO TUM KONAKE HARA
    KISKE BALA HARI NAAM BISAARA
    JEETE JEEKE NA TE HAI

3   LAKH CHO RAASI BHOOGATA KE BHAIYE
    BAROO BHAAGYA MANUSHA TAN PAAYE
    KIS PAR BHEE KACHU KAREE NA KAMAAYEE
    JAB LEKHA MANGE NA SAYEE

    SHREE RAAM JAYA RAAM JAYA JAYA RAAM OM

    DAI DEVA SA NAHEE AATE HAI JINA
    PHIR PEECHE PACHTA TE HAI JINA

MEANING

1   The days are passing away speedily.
    Remember the holy name of Sri Rama, remember God.
    Give up all the worldly and sensual enjoyments.
    Whatever you sow you shall reap.
    When you die you will take not one penny.

2   Brothers, friends, relatives and family members
    all these are related to you as long as you are alive.
    Otherwise 'whose are you' and 'who is yours'?
    What power has caused you to forget the Name of God.

3   After passing through 840,000 births in different species,
    you have found this human life with great fortune.
    In spite of that you are not gaining any merit.
    When God will ask for an explanation, what will you tell him?
    No one will come to your help.
    So repent and save yourself.

RAADHE KRISHNA BOAL

RAGA - Pilu   TAL - Keherwa

1 RAADHE KRISHNA BOAL MUKHA SAY
   RAADHE KRISHNA BOAL MUKHA SAY
   RAADHE KRISHNA BOAL TAIRO
   KYA LAGE GA MOUL, AH TAIRO

2 HAATHA PAVANAHI HILANA
   DAS BEESA KOUS NAHI CHALANA
   TOO MAN KEE DHOONDEE KHOUL TAIRO
   KYA LAGE GA MOUL, AH TAIRO

3 RAADHE KRISHNA BOAL MUKHA SAY
   SHREE RAAM JAYA RAAM JAYA JAYA RAAM OM

   G R S M G R S / P M G R S / N S G M P / M P G M P M P
   SHREE

   S N D P M P / N N D P M P / DP M P G M P G M G R S SHREE
   R

   G R S M G R S / P M G R S / N S G M P / M P G M P M P
   S N D P M P N N D P M P D P M P G M P G M G R S SHREE
   RAA

   KYA LAGE GA MOUL, AH TAIRO
   RAADHE KRISHNA BOAL

   KOUN BACHANA DE AAYAA
   ISA MAIYA MEN LALCHAYAA
   TOO MAN KE AKHAY KHUL TAIRO
   KYA LAGE GA MOUL, AH TAIRO

MEANING

1 Open your mouth and chant Radha Krishna
   Have no reservation because it does not cost you anything

2 While chanting the name of Radha Krishna,
   you do not have to move your hand and foot,
   you need not walk 10-20 miles and be exhausted
   Open your heart and mind and chant the name of Radha Krishna.

3 You are allured in Maya.
   Before birth you begged God to liberate you
   and promised you will remember him.
   Now you should open the eyes of your mind
   and remember god for it cost you nothing but you will get everything.

SACHO TERO RAAMA NAAM

RAGA - Pilu   TAL - Keherwa

1   SACHO TERO RAAMA NAAM
    SACHO TERO KRISHNA NAAM
    JUTHE JAGA ME KAAMA DAAM
    SACHO TERO RAAMA NAAM

2   KYA LEKE TU AAYAA JAGA ME
    KYA LEKE TUM JAOGE
    MUTTHI BANDHE KE AYETHE
    AURA HAATHA PASAARE JAOGE
    SACHO TERO RAAMA NAAM....

3   GANGAA JAMUNAA TIRATHA KI NAHI
    MATHE TILAKA LAGAYO
    SAARI DUNIYA PHIRATA BAAWARI
    HARI KAA BHEDA NA PAAYO
    SACHO TERO.....

4   NYAAYYA DHARMA KE STAMBAA ME BAADHE
    VYAKULA HUVE KABIR
    MAALAKA JAANE KAUNA CHALAVE
    SANGA NA JAATE SARIRA
    SACHO TERO.....

MEANING

1   The only reality or truth is the name of God.
    This illusory world is a place of desire and pain.

2   When you came what did you bring with you?
    What will you take with you when you go?
    You came with your fist closed (empty).
    Everything will slip out of your hands when you leave.
    Your hands will remain open when you go.

3   You have made pilgrimage to the Ganges and Yamuna.
    You have made Tilak on your forehead and
    you have roamed around the whole world,
    but you have not found out the secret of the Lord.

4   I am bound up by justice and righteousness,
     so I am very much unhappy to see you in this state.
    Only God knows who directs the whole world,
     but this body will not accompany you at the end.

SAMAJHE MANAA

RAGA - Bhairavi   TAL - Tintal

1   SAMAJHE MANAA KOYEE RE NAHEE APANAA
    NIS DIN RAAM NAAM JAPA NAA RE
    SAMAJHE MANAA

2   SAMAJHE MANAA KOYEE NAHEE APANAA
    KHAALI AANAA KHAALI JAANAA
    DHAN YOWVAN KA NAHEE THEKAANAA
    YE DUNIYA DODIN KAA MELAA
    NAA TU KISSEE KAA NAA KOYEE TERAA
    JIVAN HAI DIN CHARU BANDHE

3   DOULAT DUNIYAA SUKHA SABA SAMPATA
    SABA SAPANA RE
    NIS DIN RAAM NAAM JAPA NAA RE

4   BHAI BANDHU AUR KUTUMBA PARIVAARA
    SABA APA APANAA MATALABAWALA
    AAPA GAYE PEECHHE DUBA GAYI DUNIYA

5   KAHATA KABIR SUNO BHAIYE SADHO
    NIS DIN RAAMA NAAM JAPA NAA RE
    SAMAJHE.....

MEANING

1   Understand Oh mind that nobody is your own.
    So you should chant every day and night Rama's Name.

2   Understand oh mind that wealth and youth are not going to remain forever.
    This world is only a festival of two days.
    You do not belong to anybody and nobody belongs to you.
    This life of yours is only for four days.

3   The wealth and happiness of the world is all a dream.
    Every day repeat the name of Rama.
    Only God's name is real.

4   All the family members, brothers and friends are all selfish.
    When you are gone the world is gone.

5   Saint Kabir says: listen, O brother,
    every day repeat the name of Rama.

EKA DIN JAANAA RE BHAAI

RAGA - Pilu   TAL - Keherwa

EKA DIN JAANAA RE BHAAI
KABHI NA KABHI JAANAA RE BHAAI
SAB SE RAAM BHAJAN KARA LE
EK DIN JAANAA RE BHAAI

1   PAAPA KAPATA KARA MAAYAA JODI
    GARWA KARE DHANA KA JAGATA ME
    SABHI CHODA KARA CHALAA MUSAAPHIR
    VASANA VAA DANA KA
    JAGATA ME JAANAA RE BHAAI
    EK DIN JAANAA RE BHAAI

2   SUNDAR KAAYAA DEKHA LO BHAIE
    LODA KARE TANA KA BHAIE
    CHHUTA SWAASA BIKARAA GAYI DEHI
    JIVAN MAALAA MANA KAA
    JAGATA ME JAANAA RE BHAAI
    JAGATA ME JAANAA RE BHAAI

3   YOWVANA NAARI LAGE PIYAARI
    MOWJA KARE MANA KA BHA I
    MOWJA KARE MANAKA BHAI
    KAALA BALIKAA LAGE TAMASA
    BHULAA JAAYE TANA KAA
    JAGATA ME JAANAA RE BHAAI
    JAGATA ME JAANAA RE BHAAI

4   JAHAN SAMSAARAA SWAPNA KI MAAYAA
    MELAA PAALA CHINA KA BHAI
    MELA PAALA CHINA KA BHAAI
    KAHATA KABIR SUNO BHAI SADHO
    APA GAYE PICHHE DUBA GAYI DUNIYA
    RAAM BHAJAN KARA LE
    EK DIN.........

MEANING

At any moment you may have to leave this world O Brother.
Therefore you should do Bhajans of Ram.

1   Oh Brother, one day for sure you will have to go
    and everything will be left here.
    The only thing that will go with you is Rama's name.
    You are attached to sin and deception.
    You are proud of your wealth not realizing that
    you are only a traveller in this world and nothing belongs to you.
    You will leave everything when you go.

2   The beautiful body itself is the source of unhappiness.
    You pamper it but when the breath leaves you the body fades away.

3   You like to love the young women and indulge in the pleasures of the
    world and
    your mind thinks it is happy.
    Give up this body consciousness and learn the
    lesson from the world that everything is transitory.

4   The whole world is an illusion.
    It is an affair of only a moment.
    Kabir says when you are gone the world is gone.
    You have a short time so sing God's name.
    When the ego is removed you are liberated.

AAMANA MOHAN MURALI VALAA

RAGA - Durga   TAL - Tintal

AAMANA MOHAN MURALI VALAA
MURALI VALAA SAKHI HAI KAALAA
AAMANA MOHAN MURALI VALA A
MURALI VALAA SAKHI HAI KAALAA
AAMANA MOHAN MURALI VALAA

AAMANA NISA DINA JAKO DHYAANA DHARATA HOO
NISA DINA JAKO DHYANA DHAARATA HOO
MUNI NIGAMA GAMA GUNA GAVATA HAI
JITA JAI E UTA HAMA DEKHATA HAI
MURALI VALAA SAKHI HAI KALA / MOHAN MURALI VALAA

S R M P / R M P D / M P D S / P D S
MOHAN MURALI   .

S R / D S / P D / M P / R M / P M / R M / R S
MOHAN MURALI

S R M M R M R S / R M P P M P M P R /
M P D D P D P M / P D S S D S D P /
S R D S / P D M P / R M P M / R M R S
MOHAN MURALI

P D S S D S D P / M P D D P D P M / R M P P M P M R /
S R M M R M R S / S R M P / R M P D / M P D S P D S
MOHAN MURALI WALA

MEANING

The flute player Krishna is very attractive.
Oh Friend, the flute player is very dark.
The Yogis meditate on him all the time.
I also meditate on him day and night.
The Yogis praise this Supreme God all the time.
Wherever I go I see the flute player Krishna
the dark coloured Krishna.

TARANA

UDATANA DRITANA NA TOM TANA NA NA NA NA
UDATANA NITARE TADARE TADARE DANI
DIRA DIRA TANA DIRA DIRA TANA DRITANA DERE NA
DRITANA DRITANA TANA NA NA DERE NA
S R M P R M P D M P DS PD S S R D S P D M P R M P M R M R S
TAK TAK TAK TAK DHIRE KITA DHIRE KITA
DHIT TA GINA DHA TAGA DHIRE GANA GINA DHA
DHUMA KITA GADA GINA KATA GANA GINA DHA
DHUMAKITA GADA GINA KATA GADA GINA DHA
DHUMA KITA GADA GINA KATA GADA GINA DHA
TAG DILANG DHIRA KITA TAKA GADA GINA
TITI KATA GADA GINA DHA / TITI KATAGADA GINA DHA
TITI KATA GADA GINA
UDATANA.....

FROM JOY I CAME,

RA GA - Darbari Kanada   TAL - Dadra

FROM JOY I CAME,
FOR JOY I LIVE,
IN BLISSFUL JOY I MELT AGAIN

OM ANANDA AH ANANDA (THE BLISS OF GOD)

The Great Rishi, Bhrigu, from the Taittiriya Upanishad, went to his father Varuna and asked him to teach him of Brahman. His father told him to first learn about food, breath, eye, ear, speech, and mind; then seek to know that from which these are born, by which they live for which they search and to which they return and that is Brahman. Bhrigu meditated and fond that food is Brahman. From food are born all creatures, by food they grow, and to food they return.

Wanting to know more, Bhrigu went again to his father and asked him to teach him more of Brahman. His father told him to seek it in meditation. Bhrigu meditated and fond that Life is Brahman. In this manner Bhrigu went several times to Varuna for frther instrctions and each time his father told him to seek it in meditation, Until he experienced the highest truth that Joy is Brahman. From joy are born all creatures, for joy they live and to blissful joy they return. Those who realize that they came from joy (God) And that they are here to enjoy this creatron, then withot a dobt, they will return to Joy (God).

RULES OF RAGA BAGESHREE

RAGA - Bageshree   TAL - Jhaptal

GAA WO BAGESHREE / MRI DU LA GA TA SURA GA NEE
KA RA HA RAA PEYA THAATA / TEEWARA KARATA DHAREE
GAA WO BAGESHREE

MAA DHA MA KA REE JAA NA / SURA VAA RAY SA MA NA
PANCHA MA KA REE ALPA
M G R S N S D N S / NSGMDNSNDPDNDMGMGRS
GAA WO BAGESHREE

MEANING

Sing the Raga Bageshree / M G N is Komal or Minor, sweet and soft notes
D R is Teevara or Major / It is derived from the Thaatha Kaphi
M is the soul or main raga note (Wadi) / S is second in importance (samvadi) P is used very little

BOAL RAY

RAGA - Bageshree   TAL - Tin Tal

    BOAL RAY BOOLA RAY
    BOOLA RAY MA DHU BANA MAY MURALIYA

1   TOE CHUPA HAI TOE DUNIYA CHUP HAI
    KOYAL HAR JAMUNA KEE
    TADA PAR RAHEE HAI KUNJA KUNJA MAI
    AAJ CHAMAK CHANDA KEE
    JAAJ JARA / JAAJ JARA
    JAAJ JARA / YEA BRIJ KAY KOYALI YAA
    BOAL RAY....

2   BHOOLEE KAHANI YADA JAYEA
    EISEE TAAN SUNADAY
    DUK KAY BADAL HATA DAY MAYRA
    CHAAND MUGHAY DEKHA LADAY
    BHOOL GAIYEA / BHOOL GAIYEA
    BHOOL GAIYEA KYO MAYREE GALIYEA
    BOAL RAY

    N S G M G R S / N S G M D N D M G M G M G R S / BOAL
    RAY
    N S G M D N S N D P D N D M G M G M G R S / BOAL RAY
    M G M G R S / N D N D M G R S / S N D M G R S / BOAL RAY

MEANING

    In the forest of Madhubar, the flute sings.

1   If you are silent, then the whole world is silent.
    You are the nightingale of the Jamuna River.
    The moonlight is tormenting from forest to forest.
    Please awake Nightingale of the Jamuna River.

2   So we can remember this forgotten story.
    Sing in such a rhythm.
    Remove the clouds of my misery and show me the beautiful moon.
    Why have you forgotten my lanes.

SHREE RAMA CHANDRA

RAGA - Bageshree   TAL - Rupaka

    (See Bhajan 2 Page81)

SADHU GOVINDA KAY GUNA GAAVO

RAGA - Bageshree   **TAL** - Kherava

SADHU GOVINDA KAY GUNA GAAVO

1   MAANUSH JANAM AMOLAKA PAAYO
    VRITHAA KAAHAY GAVAAYO.

2   PATIT PUNEET EKA DEEN BANDHU HARI
    SHARANA TAA HAI TUM AAVO.

3   TAJ ABHIMANA MOHA MAAYAA TUM
    BHAJANA RAAM CHITTA LAAVO.

MEANING

Oh holy man! Chant the name and glory of God.

1   You have got a human birth which is a
    priceless gift. Why do you spend it uselessly?

2   He alone who is the purifier of the poor and
    the brother of the humble, you should surrender
    yourself to him.

3   Give up arrogance, attachment and illusion
    and bring Raamís name closer to your heart.

NAMO AADIRUPA

RAGA - Vrindavan Saranga   **TAL** - Kherava

SHLOKA

TWAMEVA MAATA CHAPITA TWAMEVA
TWAMEVA BANDHU CHASAKHA TWAMEVA
TWAMEVA VIDYA DRAVINAM TWAMEVA
TWAMEVA SARVAM MAMADEVAA

MEANING

Oh lord thou art my mother, thou art my father
Thou art my friend, thou art my relative
Thou are my learning, thou art my intellect,
My all thou art

BHAJAN

NAMO AADIRUPA OMKARASVARUPA
VISHVACHIYA BAPA SRI PANDURANGA

1. TUJIYA SATTENE TUJE GUNA GAVU
   TENE SUKHI RAHU SARVA KAALA   (NAMO)

2. TUNCHI VAKTA JNANASI ANJANA
   SARVA HONE JANE TUJYA HAATI   (NAMO)

3. TUKA MHANE JETHE NAHI MI TU PANA
   STAVAVETEN KONA KONA LAGI   (NAMO)

MEANING

I bow to Thee the Primeval Form, the Swarupa of Om.
O Panduranga, the Father of the Universe (I bow to Thee)

1. O God, whenever I am given the opportunity
   to sing Thy praise I am happiest.

2. Thou art the giver of real knowledge.
   Everything is in Thy hands.

3. Tuka says, "When 'I'-ness and 'Thy'-ness are lost,
   who can praise whom?

PAGA GUNGHURA BHAANDA

RAGA - Malkouns   TAL - Tintal

HARI OM, HARI OM, HARI OM,

PAGA GHUNGHURU BAANDHA MEERAA NAACHEE RE
MEERAA NAACHEE RE, MEERAA NAACHE RE

1. VISH KAA PYAALAA RAANAA JEE BHEJAA
   PEEBATA MEERAA HAANSEE RE
   LOGA KAHE MEERAA BHAEE BAAVAREE
   SAASA KAHE KULA NAASHEE RE

2. SAAMPA PITAARAA RAANAA JEE BHEJAA
   NAVA LAKHA HAAR KAR PAHANAA RE
   MEERAA KAHE PRABHU GIRIDHAR NAAGARA
   AAPA HEE HOGAI DAASEE RE

MEANING

Meera was a sixteenth century Rajput Princess. One day a wedding procession passed by the palace and she asked her mother what was happening. Her mother told her it was a bride groom going for his bride. When Meera asked when her bride groom was coming, her mother took her to a statue of Krishna and said that *he* was her bride groom. From then on Miraa worshiped Krishna as her beloved. Following tradition, when she came of age, she was married to a prince. She told the prince she was already married to Krishna, but she would fulfill her earthly duties as his wife.

Meera's inlaws were Shaivites, so they built her a temple outside the courtyard where she could have her Krishna Murti. Everyday she would go to the temple to blissfully sing with the yogi's, saints, and devotees. Eventually the prince's family became mortified by her behavior because singing and dancing with common folk was not befitting of a princess. But Miraa loved the association of God intoxicated devotees and would not be dissuaded. The disgrace to the prince's family soon became so great that they decided to kill her. They tried by sending her a cobra in a basket, telling her it was a garland for Krishna. She offered it to Krishna and when she opened the basket it had become a garland. Then they brought arsenic and told her it was milk. She offered it first to Krishna and then drank it. Just as the cobra was transformed to a garland, the poison became nectar.

When she became aware that they were trying to kill her, she decided to jump off a cliff. As she neared the precipice, the hand of Krishna reached out and held her back. He said her relationship to her husband and family was over and that now she was free. Meraa then went wandering about India singing his name in ecstasy. Her devotion was so powerfull that hundreds of songs poured from her spontaneously. Her songs are known as "Miraa Bhajans," and are sung all over India to this day.

At last she came to Vrindavan, the childhood home of Krishna. Many people, including her husband, were so taken by her devotion, that they travelled there from all over India to become her disciples. One morning the villagers heard such divine singing that they rushed into the temple. All they could see was the last peice of her sari merge into the statue of Krishna. She and her beloved Lord had become one.

HE PRABHU POORAN

RAGA - Asavari   TAL - TinTal

1   HE PRABHU POORAN NAATH HAMAARAY.
    KOWN KOWN GUNA KAHAY TUMHAARAY
    KOWN KOWN GUNA KAHAY TUMHAARAY

2   DAYAA TEREE PRABHU APARAMPAARA
    TOO HEE PRABHU HAI DAYAA BHANDHAARA

MEANING

Oh Perfect Lord our beloved Master
Who knows of your virtues?

Your mercy and compassion Oh Lord is imcomparable
You alone,dear God are the source of mercy and compassion.

MOHAY LAAGEE LAGARA GURU

RAGA - Kafi -   TAL - Tin Tal

MOHAY LAAGEE LAGANA GURU CHARANANA KEE
MOHAY LAAGEE LAGANA GURU CHARANANA KEE

1   CHARANA BINAA MOHAY KACHHU NAHEE BHAAVAY
    JHOOTH MAAYAN MOHAY SAPANANA KEE

2   BHAVA SAAGAR SAB SOOKHA GAYO HAI
    FIKAR NAHEE MOHAY TARANANA KEE
    MEERAA KAHAY PRABHU GIRIDHAR NAAGAR
    ULATA BHAYO MOHAY NAYANANA KEE

MEANING

I have found great joy at the feet of the Guru

1   Apart from your holy company I have no other interest
    The truth dawns on me that this world is transitory like a dream

2   The pleasures of the world no longer interest me
    I have no anxiety of overcoming the difficulties of life
    Meera says she is satisfied
    having experienced the vision of Lord Krishna.

AARAY MAN RAAM

RAGA - Bheempalasi   TAL - Ektal

AARAY MAN RAAM NAAM
TOO JAPA JAPA

AUR TOE SADHANA
NAHEE AH JAGAME
YOGA YOGA

SHREE RAAM CHANDRA KRIPALU BHAJAMAN

(See Bhajan 2 Pg. 81)

RAGA - Kafri   TAL - Tin Tal

MANUWA RAMA NAMA RASA PEEJE

MANUWA RAMA NAMA RASA PEEJE

1. TYAJA KUSANGA SATSANGA BAITHA NITA
    HARI CHARACHA SUNA LIJE
    MANUWA

2. KAMA KRODHA MADA LOBHA MOHAKO
    BAHA CHITTASE DEEJE
    MIRAKE PRABHU GIRIDHARA NAGAR
    TAHIKE RANGAMEN BHEEJE
    MANUWA

MEANING

oh! man enjoy this bliss of reciting
the sweet name of ramachandra.

1. keep away from bad society and
    be seated with holy company.
    always hear the spiritual discourses and stories of god.

2. drive out from the mind impurities of
    lust, anger, pride, greed, dilusion and other pasions.
    color your mind with the thought of giridhara nagar,
    who is the lord of mirabai.
    oh! man enjoy the bliss of reciting the sweet name of rama.

BHAJMAN RAAM CHARAN SUKHADAIYEE

RAGA - Desh   TAL - Kherava

(See Adorations to Raama Pg. 105)

BHAJO RAY BHAIYAA

RAGA - Bhairavy   TAL - Kherava

BHAJO RAY BHAIYAA
RAAMA GOVINDA HAREE

1. JAPA TAPA SAADHANA
   KACCHU NAHI LAAGAT
   KHARACHATA NAHI GATHAREE.

2. SANTATA SAMPATA SUKHA KAY KAARAN
   JAASAY BHOOL PAREE.

3. KAHATA KABEERA JAA MUKHA RAAMA NAHI
   WOE MUKHA DHOOLA BHAREE.

MEANING

Oh Brother sing the name of Raama, Govinda and Hari.

1. Japa, tapa and saadhana (spiritual practice) costs nothing.
   You don't have to spend from your stored wealth
   to sing the glory of God.

2. Don't forget him the Great One
   who is the source of perpetual happiness and prosperity.

3. The poet and saint Kabir says that
   that person in whose mouth the name of god does not enter
   is fit to be filled with mud

CHANTS

HARE RAAMA HARE RAAMA RAAMA RAAMA HARE HARE
HARE KRISHNA HARE KRISHNA KRISHNA KRISHNA HARE HARE

JAYA JAYA RAAMA

RAGA - Todi   TAL - Kherava

JAYA JAYA RAAMA JAYA RAGHU RAAMA
SEETAA RAAMA SHREE RAGHU RAAMA - JAYA JAYA RAAMA
JAYA RAGHU RAAMA.

1 PASHUPATI RANJANA PAAVANA RAAMA
   PAAPA VIMOCHANA TAARAKA RAAMA.

2 NAVA NAVA KOMALA MAYGHA SHYAAMA
   BHAYA HARNA BHADRAA CHALA RAAMA

3 DASHARATHA NANDANA HE PARAM DHAAMA
   DASHA MUKHA MAAR DHANA SHREE RAGHU RAAMA

MEANING

Victory to Raama Victory to Rama of the Raghu family.
Victory to Seeta and Raama.

1 The Great purifier Raama pleases his entire creation.
   You are the one who frees us from Pain and
   take us accross the ocean of miseries.

2 The generous and mercifull Raama frees us from fear
   and brings us prosperity and joy.

3 Oh Beloved Son of King Dasharatha, The Highest Abode
   Oh Raghu Raama you are the one who destroyed Ravana
   the one of ten heads, representing the extrovert senses.

CHANTS

SHREE RAAM JAI RAAM JAI JAI RAAM OM
SHREE RAAM JAI RAAM JAI JAI RAAM OM

SHRI HANUMAAN CHALISA

MANTRA
    SHRI GANESHAYA NAMAH
    SHRI HANUMATE NAMAH

SHLOKA

1. SRI GURU CARANA SAROJA RAJA
   NIJA MANU MUKURU SUDHARI
   BARANA UN RAGHU BARA BIMALA JASU
   JO DAYAKU PHALA CARI

2. BUDDHI HINA TANU JANIKE
   SUMIRAUN PAVANA KUMARA
   BALA BUDDHI BIDYA DEHU MOHIN
   HARAHU KALESA BIKARA

MEANING

1. With the dust of the Guru's lotus feet, I first clean
the mirror of my heart and mind and then narrate the sacred
glory of Shri Rama Chandra, the supreme among the Raghu dynasty,
which gives the four fruits of life.

2. Knowing myself to be ignorant, I urge you, O Hanuman,
son of Pavana (the wind God) O Lord, bestow on me strength,
wisdom and knowledge and take away all my suffering and sins.

1. JAYA HANUMANA JNANA GUNA SAGARA
   JAYA KAPISA TIHUN LOKA UJAGARA

2. RAMA DUTA ATULITA BALA DHAMA
   ANJANI PUTRA PAVANA SUTA NAMA

3. MAHABIRA BIKRAMA BAJA RANGI
   KUMATI NIVARA SUMATI KE SANGI

4. KANCANA BARANA BIRAJA SUBESA
   KANANA KUNDALA KUNCITA KESA

5. HATHA BAJRA AU DHVAJA BIRAJAI
   KANDHE MUNJA JANE U SAJAL

6. SANKARA SUVANA KESARI NANDANA
   TEJA PRATAPA MAHA JAGA BANDANA

7. VIDYAVANA GUNI ATI CATURA
   RAMA KAJA KARIBE KO ATURA

8. PRABHU CARITRA SUNIBE KO RASIYA,
   RAMA LASANA SITA MANA BASIYA

9. SUKSMA RUPA DHARI SIYAHIN DIKHAVA
   BIKATA RUPA DHARI LANKA JARAVA

10. BHIMA RUPA CHARI ASURA SANHARE
    RAMA CANDRA KE KAJA SANVARE

11. LAYA SAJIVANA LAKHANA JIYAYE
    SRI RAGHUBIRA HARASI URA LAYE

12. RAGHU PATI KINHI BAHUTA BADAI
    TUMA MAMA PRIYA BHARATA SAMA BHA-I

13. SAHASA BADANA TUMHARO JASA GAVAIN
    ASA KAHI SRI PATI KANTHA LAGAVAIN

14. SANAKADIKA BRAHMADI MUNISA
    NARADA SARADA SAHITA AHISA

15. JAMA KUBERA DIGAPALA JAHAN TE
    KABI KOBIDA KAHI SAKE KAHAN TE

16. TUMA UPAKARA SUGRIVAHIN KINHA
    RAMA MILAYA RAJA PADA DINHA

17. TUMHARO MANTRA BIBHISANA MANA
    LANKESVARA BHA-E SABA JAGA JANA

18. JUGA SAHASRA JOJANA PARA BHANU
    LILYO TAHI MADHURA PHALA JANU

19. PRABHU MUDRIKA MELI MUKHA MAHIN
    JALADHI LANGHI GAYE ACARAJA NAHIN

20. DURGAMA KAJA JAGATA KE JETE
    SUGAMA ANUGRAHA TUMHARE TETE

21. RAMA DU-ARE TUMA RAKHAVARE
    HOTA NA AJNA BINU PAISARE

22. SABA SUKHA LAHAI TUMHARI SARANA
    TUMA RACCHAKA KAHU KO DARA NA

23. APANA TEJA SAMHARO APAI
    TINON LOKA HANKA TEN KANPAI

24. BHUTA PISACA NIKATA NAHIN AVAI
    MAHABIRA JABA NAMA SUNAVAI

25. NASAI ROGA HARAI SABA PIRA
J   APATA NIRANTARA HANUMATA BIRA

26. SANKATA TEN HANUMANA CHUDAVAI
    MANA KRAMA BACANA DHYANA JO LAVAI

27. SABA PARA RAMA TAPASVI RAJA
    TINA KE KAJA SAKALA TUMA SAJA

28. AURA MANORATHA JO KO-I LAVAI
    SO-I AMITA JIVANA PHALA PAVAI

29. CARON JUGA PARATAPA TUMHARA
    HAI PARA SIDDHA JAGATA UJIYARA

30. SADHU SANTA KE TUMA RAKHAVARE
    ASURA NIKANDANA RAMA DULARE

31. ASTA SIDDHI NAU NIDHI KE DATA
    ASA BARA DINA JANAKI MATA

32. RAMA RASAYANA TUMHARE PASA
    SADA RAHO RAGHU PATI KE DASA

33. TUMHARE BHAJANA RAMA KO PAVAI
    JANAMA JANAMA KE DUKHA BISARAVAI

34. ANTA KALA RAGHUBARA PURA JA-I
    JAHAN JANMA HARI BHAKTA KAHA-I

35. AURA DEVATA CITTA NA DHARA-I
    HANUMATA SE-I SARBA SUKHA KARA-I

36. SANKATA KATAI MITAI SABA PIRA
    JO SUMIRAI HANUMATA BALA BIRA

37. JAI JAI JAI HANUMANA GOSA-IN
    KRPA KARAHU GURU DEVA KI NA-IN

38. JO SATA BARA PATHA KARA KO-I
    CHUTAHI BANDI MAHA SUKHA HO-I

39. JO YAHA PADHAI HANUMANA CALISA
    HOYA SIDDHI SAKHI GAURISA

40. TULASIDASA SADA HARI CERA
    KI JAI NATHA HRDAYA MAHAN DERA

MEANING

1. Glory to you, O Hanuman, ocean of all knowledge and virtue.
   Victory to you, lord of the monkeys, enlightener of the three worlds.

2. The messenger of Shri Rama and the abode of imeasurable
   strength, you are known also as Anjaniputra and Pavana suta
   (son of Anjani Mata and Pavana).

3. Mighty, powerful and strong as lightning, O Mahavira, O
   great hero, you, the companion of wisdom, dispel all my
   dark and evil thoughts.

4. O golden hued Hanuman, you look beautiful with your
   shining earrings and curly hair.

5. You hold the mace of lightning and a flag of victory in
   your hands, with the sacred thread of munja grass adorning your shoulder.

6. Incarnation of Lord Shankara and the delight of Keshari (your
   earthly father, the monkey chief), your great luster and glory
   are praised by the whole world.

7. The master of all knowledge, full of virtue and wisdom,
   you are always eager to serve Lord Rama.

8. With Rama, Lakshmana and Sita in your heart, you
   delight in listening to the Lord's holy acts.

9. After presenting your minute, subtle form to Mother Sita,
   you assumed a huge size and burnt the city of Lanka.

10. Taking a colossal form, you killed the demons and thus
    accomplished all of Shri Ramas missions.

11. You brought the life giving sanjivani herb which revived Lakshmana,
    and Shri Rama embraced you joyfully.

12. Shri RamaChandra praised you most highly and declared
    you were as dear to him as his brother Bharata.

13. Shri Rama, the lord of Lakshmi, embraced you fondly, stating that
    even the thousand headed serpent, Shesha Naga, sings your glory.

14. Sanaka and his brothers, Brahma and the other gods, high sages,
    Narada, Sharada and Shesha Naga (the serpent king) eternally sing your
    praise.

15. What to speak of poets and seers? Even Yama (the god of death), Kubera
    (the god of wealth) and the dikpalas (guardian deities) have no words to
    praise your glory.

16. You gave great service to Sugriva, introducing him to Shri
    Rama who blessed him and restored him to the throne.

17. Vibhishana accepted your advice and became the king of Lanka,
    as the whole world knows.

18. You swallowed the sun millions of miles away,
    taking it to be a sweet fruit.

19. Carrying the Lord's ring in your mouth, you jumped over the
    mighty ocean. There is little wonder in that (considering your
    other marvelous deeds).

20. By your grace, all the tasks of the world, howsoever difficult,
    are rendered easy to accomplish.

21. You are the gate keeper of Shri Rama's kingdom
    which no one can enter without your consent.

22. One who takes refuge in you enjoys all happiness and,
    with you as protector, has no need of fear.

23. You alone are able to control your energy and might.
    Before your deafening roar, all the three worlds tremble.

24. Evil spirits cannot come near the devotee who
    chants your name, O Mahavira.

25. All diseases are destroyed and all pains vanish when your powerful
    name is repeated constantly with love and devotion, O Hanuman.

26. Hanuman keeps free from calamity those who meditate
    on him with thought, word and deed.

27. You successfuly accomplished all the missions of Lord Rama,
    who fulfills the divine desires of devotees who engage in penance.

28. Along with whatever other desire the devotee may have, he will
    receive the imperishable fruit (realization of the highest reality)
    by devotion to you.

29. Your glory is acclaimed in the four yugas (cosmic ages) and
    your radiance is spread throughout the cosmos.

30. Shri Rama has great affection for you, O mahavira,
    destroyer of demons and protector of the saints.

31. You are blessed by Mother Sita (daughter of Janaki) to grant anyone
    any of the eight siddhis and nine nidhis.

32. With the ambrosia of devotion to Shri Rama, you are always in
the service of the Lord.

33. Chanting your name, one can reach Shri Rama and become
free from the sufferings of many lives.

34. At the end of a lifespan of such devotion, one enters Raghuvara, the eternal abode of Shri Rama, and is known there as a devotee of Lord Hari.

35. All happiness is granted to the devotee who serves you, O Hanuman,
even if he does not worship any other god.

36. All difficulties and suffering are taken away from those
who contemplate the all powerful Shri Hanuman.

37. Glory, glory, all glory to you, O Hanuman. Be as gracious
and compassionate to me as my Guru, my supreme teacher.

38. He who chants this prayer a hundred times is liberated from
all earthly bondage and enjoys the highest bliss.

39. He who reads this Hanumana Chalisa attains perfection, as Shiva,
the lord of Gauri is the witness.

40. Tulasidasa (the writer of these verses), who is eternally the servant of
Lord Hari, prays for Lord Hanuman to take residence in his heart forever.
is known there as a devotee of Lord Hari.

ALI MAN LAGI RE

RAGA - Yaman Kalyan   TAL - Kherava

TAL: KEHERWA

1. ALI MAN LAGI RE BRINDAVANA NIKO
   GHARA GHARA TULASI THAKURA PUJA
   DARASHANA GOVINDAJI KO

2. NIRAMALA NIRA BAHATA JAMUNA KO
   BHOJANA DUKHA DAHI KOOO
   RATHANA SIMHASANA AAPA BIRAJI
   TILAKA DHARO TULASI KO

3. KUNJANA KUNJANA PHIRATA RADHIKA
   SHABADA SUMATA MURALI KOOO
   MIRA KE PRABHO GIRADHAR NAJAR
   BHAJANA BINA NARA PIKO

MEANING

1. Oh mind, take refuge in Krishna of Vrindavan.
   In every home there is worship of God and the Tulsi tree
   for the vision of Govind.

2. In the Jamuna river flows pure water
   Sing the glory of the Lord who removes pain.
   You dwell on the jewelled seat of the Lion
   and wear the tilak of Tulsi.

3. Radhika wanders in all the streets
   And listens to the word of Murali.
   MeeraŌs Lord is Krishna,
   Without devotion to him there is no peace.

BHAJA GOVINDAM

1. BHAJA GOVINDAM, BHAJA GOVINDAM
   GOVINDAM BHAJA MOODHAMATE
   SAMPRAAPTE SANNIHITE KAALE
   NA HI NA HI RAKSHATI DUKRINYAKARANE

2. MOODHA JAHEEHI DHANAAGAMATRISHNAAM
   KURU SADBUDDHIM MANASI VITRISHNAAM
   YALLABHASE NIJAKARMOPAATTAM
   VITTAM TENA VINODAYA CHITTAM

3. NAREE STHANABHARA NAABHEEDESAM
   DRISHTVAA MAA GAA MOHAAVESAM
   ETAN MAAMSAVASAADI VIKAARAM
   MANASI VICHINTAYA VAARAM VAARAM

4. NALINEEDALAGATA JALAMATITARALAM
   TADVAJJEEVITAMATISAYA CHAPALAM
   VIDDHI VYAADHYABHIMAANAGRASTAM
   LOKAM SOKAHATAM CHA SAMASTAM

5. YAAVADVITTOPAARJANA SAKTAH
   TAAVANNIJAPARIVAARO RAKTAH
   PASCHAAJJEEVATI JARJARADEHE
   VAARTAAM KOPI NA PRICHCHATI GEHE

6. YAAVATPAVANO NIVASATI DEHE
   TAAVATPRICHCHATI KUSALAM GEHE
   GATAVATI VAAYAU DEHAAPAAYE
   BHAARYAA BIBHYATI TASMINKAAYE

7. BAALASTAAVAT KREEDAA SAKTAH
   TARUNASTAAVAT TARUNEESAKTAH
   VRIDDHASTAAVAT CHINTAASAKTAH
   PARAME BRAHMANI KOPI NA SAKTAH

8. KAA TE KAANTAA KASTE PUTRAH
   SAMSAAROYAMATEEVA VICHITRAH
   KASYA TVAM KAH KUTA AAYAATAH
   TATTVAM CHINTAYA TADIHA BHRAATAH

9. SATSANGATVE NISSANGATVAM
   NISSANGATVE NIRMOHATVAM
   NIRMOHATVE NISCHALATATTVAM
   NISCHALATATTVE JEEVANMUKTIH

10. VAYASI GATE KAH KAAMAVIKAARAH
    SUSHKE NEERE KAH KAASAARAH
    KSHEENE VITTE KAH PARIVAARO
    GYAATE TATTVE KAH SAMSAARAH

11. MAA KURU DHANAJANAYAUVANAGARVAM
    HARATI NIMESHAATKAALAH SARVAM
    MAAYAAMAYAMIDAMAKHILAM BUDDHVAA
    BRAHMAPADAM TVAM PRAVISA VIDITVAA

12. DINAYAAMINYAU SAAYAM PRAATAH
    SISIRAVASANTAU PUNARAAYAATAH
    KAALAH KREEDATI GACHCHHATYAAYUH
    TADAPI NA MUNCHATYAASAAVAAYUH

13. KAA TE KAANTAA DHANAGATACHINTAA
    VAATULA KIM TAVA NAASTI NIYANTAA
    TRIJAGATI SAJJANASAMGATIREKAA
    BHAVATI BHAVAARNAVATARANE NAUKAA

14. JATILO MUNDEE LUNCHHITAKESAH
    KAASHAAYAAMBARA BAHUKRITAVESHAH
    PASYANNAPI CHA NA PASYATI MOODHO
    HY-UDARANIMITTAM BAHUKRITAVESHAH

15. ANGAM GALITAM PALITAM MUNDAM
    DASANAVIHEENAM JAATAM TUNDAM
    VRIDDHO YAATI GRIHEETVAA DANDAM
    TADAPI NA MUNCHATYAASAAPINDAM

16. AGRE VAHNIH PRISHTHE BHAANUH
    RAATRAU CHUBUKASAMARPITAJAANUH
    KARATALABHIKSHASTARUTALAVAASAH
    TADAPI NA MUNCHATYAASAAPAASAH

17. KURUTE GANGAASAAGARAGAMANAM
    VRATAPARIPAALANAMATHAVAA DAANAM
    GYAANAVIHEENAH SARVAMATENA
    MUKTIM NA BHAJATI JANMASATENA

18. SURAMANDIRATARUMOOLANIVAASAH
    SAYYAA BHOOTALAMAJINAM VAASAH
    SARVAPARIGRAHA BHOGATYAAGAH
    KASYA SUKHAM NA KAROTI VIRAAGAH

19. YOGARATO VAA BHOGARATO VAA
    SANGARATO VAA SANGAVIHEENAH
    YASYA BRAHMANI RAMATE CHITTAM
    NANDATI NANDATI NANDATYEVA

20. BHAGAVADGEETAA KINCHIDADHEETAA
    GANGAAJALAVAKANIKAA PEETAA
    SAKRIDAPI YENA MURAARISAMARCHAA
    KRIYATE TASYA YAMENA NA CHARCHAA

21. PUNARAPI JANANAM PUNARAPI MARANAM
    PUNARAPI JANANEEJATHARE SAYANAM
    HA SAMSAARE BAHUDASTAARE
    KRIPAYAA PAARE PAAHI MURAARE

22. RATHYAACHARPATA VIRACHITAKANTHAH
    PUNYAAPUNYAVIVARJITAPANTHAH
    YOGEE YOGANIYOJITACHITTO
    RAMATE BAALONMATTAVADEVA

23. KASTVAM KOHAM KUTA AAYAATAH
    KAA ME JANANEE KO ME TAATAH
    ITI PARIBHAAVAYA SARVAMASAARAM
    VISVAM TYAKTVAA SVAPNAVICHAARAM

24. TVAYI MAYI CHAANYATRAIKO VISHNUH
    VYARTHAM KUPYASI MAYYASAHISHNUH
    BHAVA SAMACHITTAH SARVATRA TVAM
    VAANCHASYACHIRAADYADI VISHNUTVAM

25. SATRAU MITRE PUTRE BANDHAU
    MAA KURU YATNAM VIGRAHASANDHAU
    SARVASMINNAPI PASYAATMANAANAM
    SARVATROTSRIJA BHEDAAGYAANAM

26. KAAMAM KRODHAM LOBHAM MOHAM
    TYAKTVAA ATMAANAM PASYATI SOHAM
    AATMAGYAANA VIHEENAA MOODHAAH
    TE PACHYANTE NARAKANIGOODHAAH

27. GEYAM GEETAANAAMASAHASRAM
    DHYEYAM SREEPATIROOPAMAJASRAM
    NEYAM SAJJANASANGE CHITTAM
    DEYAM DEENAJANAAYA CHA VITTAM

28. SUKHATAH KRIYATE RAAMAABHOGAH
    PASCHAADDHANTA SAREERE ROGAH
    YADYAPI LOKE MARANAM SARANAM
    TADAPI NA MUNCHATI PAAPAACHARANAM

29. ARTHAMANARTHAM BHAAVAYA NITYAM
    NAASTI TATAH SUKHALESAH SATYAM
    PUTRAADAPI DHANABHAAJAAM BHEETIH
    SARVATRAISHAA VIHITAA REETIH

30. PRAANAAYAAMAM PRATYAAHAARAM
    NITYAANITYAVIVEKAVICHAARAM
    JAAPYASAMETA SAMAADHIVIDHAANAM
    KURUVAVADHAANAM MADADAVADHAANAM

31. GURUCHARANAAMBUJA NIRBHARABHAKTAH
SAMSAARAADACHIRAADBHAVA MUKTAH
SENDRIYAMAANASANIYAMAADEVAM
DRAKSHYASI NIJAHRIDAYASTHAM DEVAM

MEANING

1. Seek Govind, Seek Govind, Seek Govind, O Fool. When the appointed time comes (death), grammar rules surely will not save you.

2. O Fool! Give up the thirst to possess wealth. Create in your mind, devoid of passions, thoughts of the Reality. With whatever you get (as a reward of the past), entertain your mind (be content).

3. Seeing the full bosom of young maidens and their navel, do not fall a prey to maddening delusion. This is but a modification of flesh and fat. Think well thus in your mind again and again.

4. The water drop playing on a lotus petal has an extremely uncertain existence; so also is life ever unstable. Understand, the very world is consumed by disease and conceit, and is riddled with pangs.

5. As long as there is the ability to earn and save so long are all your dependents attached to you. Later on, when you come to live with an old, infirm body, no one at home cares to speak even a word with you.

6. As long as there dwells breath (life) in the body, so long they enquire of your welfare at home. Once the breath (life) leaves, the body decays, even the wife fears that very same body.

7. So long as one is in one's boyhood, one is attached to play; so long as one is in youth, one is attached to one's own woman (passion); so long as one is in old age, one is attached to anxiety (pang)...(Yet) no one, alas, to the Supreme Brahman, is (ever seen) attached!

8. Who is your wife? Who is your son? Supremely wonderful indeed is this samsaara. Of whom are you? From where have you come? O brother, think of that Truth here.

9. Through the company of the good, there arises non-attachment; through non-attachment there arises freedom from delusion; when there is freedom from delusion, there is the Immutable Reality; on experiencing the Immutable Reality, there comes the state of 'liberated in life'.

10. When the age (youthfulness) has passed, where is lust and its play? When water is evaporated, where is the lake? When the wealth is reduced, where are the retinue? When the Truth is realized, where is samsaara?

11. Take no pride in your possession, in the people (at your command), in the youthfulness (that you have). Time loots away all these in a moment.

Leaving aside all these, after knowing their illusory nature, realize the state of Brahman, and enter into it.

12. Day and night, dawn and dusk, winter and spring, again and again come (and depart). Time sports and life ebbs away. And yet, one leaves not the gusts of desires.

13. O Distracted one! Why worry about wife, wealth, etc.? Is there not for you the One who ordains (rules, commands)? In the three worlds it is the 'association with good people' alone that can serve as a boat to cross the sea of change (birth and death).

14. One ascetic with matted locks, one with shaven head, one with hairs pulled out one by one, another parading in his ochre robes - these are fools who, though seeing, do not see. Indeed, these different disguises or apparels are only for their belly's sake.

15. The body hs become worn out. The head has turned grey. The mouth has become toothless. The old man moves about leaning on his staff. Even then he leaves not the bundle of his desires.

16. In front the fire, at the back, the sun, late at night he sits with his knees held to his chin; he receives alms in his own scooped palm and lives under the shelter of some tree, and yet the noose of desires spares him not!

17. One may, in pilgrimage, go to where the Ganges meets the ocean, called the Gangaasaagar, or observe vows, or distribute gifts away in charity. If he is devoid of first hand experience of Truth (Gyaananam), according to all schools of thought, he gains no release, even in hundred lives.

18. Sheltering in temples, under some trees, sleeping on the naked ground, wearing a deerskin, and thus renouncing all idea of possession and thirst to enjoy, to whom will not dispassion (vairaagya) bring happiness?

19. Let one revel in Yoga or let him revel in bhoga. Let one seek enjoyment in company or let him revel in solitude away from the crowd. He whose mind revels in Brahman, he enjoys ....verily, he alone enjoys.

20. To one who has studied the Bhagavad Geeta even a little, who has sipped at least a drop of Ganges water, who has worshipped at least once Lord Murari, to him there is no discussion (quarrel) with Yama, the Lord of Death.

21. Again birth, again death, and again lying in mother's womb - this samsara process is very hard to cross over...Save me, Muraare (O Destroyer of Mura) through Thy Infinite Kindness.

22. The Yogin who wears but a godadi, who walks the path that is beyond merit and demerit, whose mind is joined in perfect Yoga with its goal, he revels (in God consciousness) and lives thereafter - as a child or as a madman.

23. Who are you? Who am I? From where did I come? Who is my mother? Who is my father? Thus enquire, leaving aside the entire world of experiences (wisdom), essenceless and a mere dreamland, born of imagination.

24. In you, in me, and in (all) other places too there is but one All-pervading Reality (Vishnu). Being impatient, you are unnecessarily getting angry with me. If you want to attain soon the Vishnu status, be equal minded in all circumstances.

25. Strive not, waste not your energy to fight against or to make friends with your enemy, friend, son or relative. Seeking the Self everywhere, lift the sense of difference (plurality) born out of ignorance.

26. Leaving desire, anger, greed, and delusion, the seeker sees in the Self, 'He am I'. They are fools who have not Self-knowledge, and they (consequently), as captives in hell, are tortured.

27. The Bhagavad Geeta and Sahasranaama are to be chanted; always the form of the Lord of Lakshmi is to be meditated upon; the mind is to be led towards the company of the good; wealth is to be distributed (shared with) the needy.

28. Very readily one indulges in carnal pleasures; later on, alas, come diseases of the body. Even though in the world the ultimate end (saranam) is death, even then man leaves not his sinful behavior.

29. 'Wealth is calamitous,' thus reflect constantly: the truth is that there is no happiness at all to be got from it. To the rich, there is fear even from his own son. This is the way of wealth everywhere.

30. The control of all activities (of life's manifestations in you), the sense withdrawel (from their respective sense objects), the reflection (consisting of discrimination between the permanent and the impermanent), along with japa and the practice of reaching the total inner silence (samaadhi) - these, perform with care...with great care.

31. O Devotee of the lotus feet of the teacher may you become liberated soon from the samsaara through the discipline of the sense organs and the mind. You will come to experience (behold) the Lord that dwells in your own heart.

BHAJ MAN NISDIN SHYAAM

RAGA - Bheempalasi

1. BHAJA MAN NISDIN SHYAAM SUNDARA
   SUKHA SAAGARA HARI SHEERA DHAAWARA

2. MORA MUKUTA SHIR KATI PEETAMBARA
   MURALI ADARA DHAR GOPA VESHA DHARA
   SAKALA JAGATA KE JEEVAN DHANA PRABHU
   KARATA KRIPA NITA NIJA BHAKTANA PARA

MEANING

1. Oh mind, meditate day and night on
   the handsome Lord with blue complexion.
   The Lord Hari is the ocean of bliss.

2. He wears on his head a crown of peacock feathers and
   a beautiful yellow cloth suround his loin
   Dressed as a cowherd he holds a flute on his lips.
   He is the Supreme Lord, vital source of
   the existence of the whole universe.
   He always bestows divine Grace on his devotees.
   Oh my mind do meditate day and night on
   the handsome Lord with blue complexion.

DARSHAN DO GHANA SHYAM NATH
(SRI NARSI MEHTA KRITAM)

SHLOKA

OM ITI JNANA VASTRENA RAGANIRNEJANIKRITAH
KARMANIDRAM PRAPANNOSMI TRAHI MAM MADHUSUDANA

MEANING

O Slayer of Madhu (Lord Krishna). protect me, who, after removing the
dust of attac ment with the duster of the wisdom of Omkara, entered into
a slumber of actions.

BHAJAN

DARSHAN DO GHANASYAM NATH MORI
AKHIYA PYASI RE

1 MAN MANDIRKI JYOTI JAGADO
  GHAT GHAT VAASI RE   (DARSAN DO. .)

2 MANDIR MANDIR MURAT TERI
  PHIR BHI NA DEKHEN SURAT TERI
  YUG BITE NA AYI MILAN KI
  POORAN MASI RE   (DARSAN DO . .)

3 DVAR DAYAKA JAB TU KHOLE
  PANCHAM SUR ME GUNGA BOLE
  ANDHA DEKHE LANGARA CHALKAR
  PAHUCHE KASHI RE   (DARSAN DO . .)

4 PANI PIKAR PYAS BUJAVU
  NAINAN KO KAISE SAMJHAV
  AAKH MICHAULI CHORO ABTO
  MANKE BASI RE   (DARSAN DO . .)

5 NIRBAL KE BAL DHAN NIRDHANKE
  TUM RAKHVARE BHAKTA JANOKEE
  TERE BHAJANME SAB KUCH PAVU
  MITE UDASI RE   (DARSAN DO . .)

6 NAM JAPE PAR TUJHE NA JANE
  UNKO BHI TOO APNA MANE
  TERI DAYAKA ANT NAHI HAI
  HE DUKH NASHI RE   (DARSAN DO . .)

7 AAJ PHAISALA TERE DVAR PAR
  MERE JIT HAI TERE HAR PAR
  HAR JIT HAI TERI MAI TO
  CHARAN UPASI RE   (DARSAN DO . .)

8   DVAAR KHARA KAISE MATVALA
    MANGE TUMSE HAR TUMHARA
    NARSI KEE YE BINTI SUNLO
    BHAKTA BILASI RE   (DARSAN DO . .)

9   LAJ NA LUTJAYE PRABHU TERI
    NATH KARO NA DAYA MAY DERI
    TINO LOK CHORKAR AAVO
    GAGAN NIVAASI RE   (DARSAN DO . .)

MEANING

O my Lord having the complexion fo the water-laden clouds, grant me Thy Darshan (show Thyself to me). My eyes are thirsty to behold Thee.

1   Keep the temple of my heart illumined. Thou art present in every heart.

2   Thou art the Moorty (Deity) in each and every temple. Still without seeing Thy face, ages have passed. The full-moon night of meeting Thee has not come.

3   When the door of Thy mercy is opened the dumb will sing in Panchama Swara (a beautiful tune); the blind will see; the lame will walk and reach Kasi.

4   Thirst can be quenched by drinking water. But how to console the eyes? Now leave the game of hide and seek. Thou art the indweller of the mind.

5   Thou art the strength of the weak and the wealth of the poor. Thou art the protector of the devotees. By worshipping Thee, I will get everything. All sorrows will be removed.

6   Some repeat Thy name, but do not know Thee. Thou maketh them also Thine (accepteth them). There is no end to mercy. Thou art the destroyer of all pains.

7   There is a strange verdict at Thy doors. On Thy defeat is my victory. Both victory and defeat are Thine. I simply worship Thy feet.

8   How long am I standing intoxicated at Thy doors and beg of Thee Thy defeat. Kindly hearken to the prayer of Narsi. Thou art affectionate to Thy devotees.

9   O lord, O master, feel not shy and delay not to show mercy to me. Leaving the three worlds, come to me. Thou dwelleth in the skies.

HAMKO PANA HAI

HAMKO PANA HAI GHANSHYAM BARI MUSHKIL SE
BINDU KA ANKHAKE KOWNEME GUJARA HOGA

1 DHARMA KI RAHAPE CHALTE HAI
   BADI AJANABI DIL
   FARZAKI HOTI HAI
    HAR CHAAL BADI MUSHKIL SE

2. DHONDHANE WALOKE
   MILA JATE HAI PRABHU LAKIN
   ANKHA KARO SARATI
   PAHA CHAN BADI MUSHKIL SE

3 HAMJO MASHAHUR HAI
   PAPI TO TU PATITA PAVAN
   ADAMI BANTA HAI
   INSAAN BADI MUSHKIL SE

4 PREMAKA JAAM PIYA JATA HAI
   SARAKO DEKHAR
   TABKANI MILTA HAI
   BHAGAWAN BADI MUSHKIL SE

HAMKO PANA HAI GHAN SHYAM BADI MUSHKIL SE
BINDU KA ANKHAKE KOWNEME GUJARA HOGA

MEANING

We have to attain Ghan Shyam with great difficulty,
Without his vision, living will be difficult.

1. Trodding the path of righteousness when in ignorance,
   Every step is taken with great difficulty
   When you have a moral obligation.

2. Seekers of reality, you will reach God
   but with great difficulty you will recognize him.

3. We are well known, you are the reformer of the evil,
   With great difficulty the soul in human body
   Becomes a true human being.

4. Love is experienced, seeing the roads,
   Then with great difficulty we realise God.

HE SARADE MA HE SARADE MA

HE SARADE MA HE SARADE MA
AJNANA TA SE HAMEN TARA DE MA

1. TU SVAR KI DEVI YE SANGITA TUJHASE
   HAR SABDA TERA HAI HARGITA TUJHASE
   HAM HAI AKHELE HAM HAI ADHURE
   TERI SARAN MEN HAME PYARADE MA

2. MUNIYO NE SAMJHI GUNIYO NE JANI
   VEDO KI BHASA PURANON KI JANI
   HAM BHI TO SAMJHE HAM BHI TO JANE
   VIDYA KA HAM KO ADHIKARA DE MA

3. TU SVETA VARNI KAMAL PE VIRAJE
   HATKON MEN VINA MUKUTA SAR PE SAJE
   MAN SE HAMARE MITA KE ANDHERE
   HAM KO UJALON KA SAMSARA DE MA

O mother Sarasvati
from darkness of ignorance, take us across
(to a world of light and knowledge)

1. You are the goddess of sound (alphabet) and
   this music has come from you.
   Every word (which is meanngful) is yours
   and every song is yours.
   We are alone, we have taken refuge in thee
   O Mother, give us your love.

2. The Munis understood and
   the Masters who have great qualities know
   these are the utterances of the Vedas and the Puranas.
   We also understand, we also know,
   grant us that authority to your knowledge.

3. You are dressed in white clothing and
   thou art seated on a lotus flower.
   In thy hands is the lute (vina) and on thy head is a crown.
   Please, from our minds remove all the darkness of ignorance.
   And take across to that world of light of knowledge.

KEMA RE VISAARI

KEMA RE VISAARI 0 VANANAA VIHAAREE
RE TAARI RAADHAA DULAAREE NE KEMA RE VISAAREE

VAGADAANI VAATE HUUN VAATADIO JOTEE
BHOOLA KEEDHEE HOYA TO HUN AASUNDE LOTI
VEGALI MUNKI NE MUNE VANANAA VIHAARI
RE TARI RAADHAA DULAAREE NE

NITYA NIRANTARA MUJA ANTARAMAAN
TUJA VAJNTARA VAAGE
KAHE NE MAARAA, NANDA DULAARAA
HAIYUN SHAANE RAACHE
TAARI MAALA HUN JAPATEE VANAMAAN
BHAMATEE AANSU SAAREE
RE TARI RAADHAA DULAAREE NE

MEANING

Why have you forgotten, oh the dweller of the forest, your beloved Radha
I am waiting for you on the tracks of the forest
If I have comitted any mistake I ask you to forgive me
My tears will wash away my mistakes
You have left your beloved Radha alone, oh the dweller of the forest

Day and night an instrument of music of your name is played in my heart.
Tell me oh krishna, oh son of Nand, why I remember you so much.
Thousands of times I have counted your name on Japa mala.
With tears I am roaming in a forest.
Krishna, why have you forgotten your dear Radha?

GAIYE GANAPAT

GAIYE GANAPATI JAGAVANDANA
SHANKAR SUVAN BHAVAANI NANDANA

1. MODAKAPRIYA MUDA MANGALA DAATAA
   VIDYAA VARIDHI BUDDHI VIDHAATAA
   SHANKAR...

2. SIDDHI SADANA GAJA VANDANA VINAYAKA
   KRIPA SINDHU SUNDAR SABALAYAK
   SHANKAR...

3. MAANGAT TULASI DAASA KARA JODATA
   BASAHI RAAMA SIYA MAANASA MORE
   SHANKAR...

MEANING

I sing about Lord of the Universe Shri Ganesha.
Who is the son of Shiva and Parvati.

1. He loves sweet rolls (called Modak)He is the giver of
   Happiness and Prosperity.
   Also the giver of Knowledge and Intelligence.
   The son of Shankar and Bhavani

2. The elephant head Lord Ganehas attained many Siddhis.
   Everyone likes this beautiful Lord Ganesh
   who is the Ocean of Mercy.

3. Tulsidas asks with folded hands to Lord Ganesh
   that Lord Rama and Sita should always be in my heart.

MANGAL MANDIR

MANGAL MANDIR KHOLO DAAYAMAYA

1. JEEVAN VANA ATI VEGE VATAVYUN
   DVARA UBHO SHISHU BHOLO
   TIMIR GAYUN NE JYOTI PRAKASHYO
   SHISHU NE URAMAN LYOLYO...DAYAAMAYA

2. NAAMA MADHUR TAMA RATYO NIRANTARA
   SHISHU SAHA PREME BOLO
   DIVYA TRUSHATUR AAVYO BAALAK
   PREMA AMEERASA DHOLO...DAYAAMAYA

MEANING

Merciful Lord please open the door to the Temple.

1. He has completed his journey of life very fast.
   The innocent child is standing at the door.

2. The darkness of night has disappeared. and the light of dawn has occured.
   Please give refuge to the child...
   Lord of mercy I am singing your sweet name day and night.
   Searching for divinity, this child has come to you.
   Bless him with the nectar of love.

NAINANA MAY NANDALAAL

NAINANA MAY NANDALAAL BA SO MORAY.
MO HA NI MURATA SAAWARI SURATA
NAINAN BANI VISHAAL BA SO MORAY.

1. ADARA SUDHARAASA MURALI RAAJATA
   UR BAIJANTEE MALAA
   CHURDA GHANDHI KA, KA TI TA TA SHOBHITA.

2. NU PURA SHA DA RA SAAL
   MEERA PRABHU SAN TAN NA SUKHA DAIYEE
   BHAKTA WATSAL GOPAL BASO.

MEANING

Oh Nandalaal, come and dwell in my eyes.
Your form is captivating,

1. Come and dwell in my huge eyes.
   I enjoy the murali with the vaijantee maala.

2. Meera says that the saints bring us joy.
   Gopal inspires the devotee with great love and devotion.

KRISHNA HARE

KRISHNA HARE SRI KRISHNA HARE
DUKHIYO KE DUKHA DOOR KARE
JAYA JAYA JAYA KRISHNA HARE

1. JAPA CHAARO TARAPHA ANDHIYAARO
   AASHA KA TU KINAARA HO
   AURO KOI NA JIVANA BHAVA DAHO
   PHIRA TU HI BEDA PARA KARE
   JAI JAI JAI KRISHNA HARE

2. TU CHA HE TO SABA KUCHA KARATI
   VISHA KO BHI AMRITA KARATE
   PURANA KARATI USAKI AASHA
   JO BHI TERA DHYAN DHARE
   JAI JAI JAI KRISHNA HARE

MEANING

Lord Hari - Sri Krishna removes
the sorrows of the unhappy ones.

1. Where all around there is darkness,
   you become the shore of hope.
   When there is none else to steer life along,
   you fulfill the hopes of anyone who reflects upon you.

2. If you wish you can do anything.
   You can render poison into nectar.
   You fulfill the wishes of one who contemplates on you.

LAGAA CHUNREE ME DAAG

LAGAA CHUNREE ME DAAG
CHHUPAA-OO KAISE, GHAR JAA-OO KAISE

1. HO GAYEE MAILEE MOREE CHUNARIYAA
   KORE BADAN SEE KOREE CHUNARIYAA
   JAAKE BAABUL SE NAZRE MILAA-OO KAISE
   GHAR JAA-OO KAISE

2. BHOOL GAYEE SAB VACHAN VIDAA KE
   KHO GAYEE MAI SASURAAL ME AAKE
   JAAKE BAABUL SE NAZRE MILAA-OO KAISE
   GHAR JAA-OO KAISE

3. KOREE CHUNARIYAA AATMAA MOREE
   MEL HAI MAAYAA JAAL
   WOH DUNIYAA MORE BAABUL KAA GHAR
   YE DUNIYAA SASURAAL
   JAAKE BAABUL SE NAZRE MILAA-OO KAISE
   GHAR JAA-OO KAISE

MEANING

My clothes have become stained.
How can I hide it
How can I go home with such stained clothes

1. My clothes have become very dirty.
   My cloth is unwashed like my unwashed body.
   How can I face my father.

2. Oh Creator I have forgotton all your teachings.
   I go lost in my inlaws home
   How con I face father

3. My spotless soul is caught in the worldly entanglements.
   The world from whence I came is God's world is my Inlaw's world.
   How will I face father with my clothes dirty.

MATHAJA JOGI

MATHAJA MATHAJA MATHAJA JOGI
PAWO PARU MI TORAY

1. PREMA BHAKTI KO PANKA HI NYARO
   HAMAKO GYLA BATAJA JOGI

2. AGARA CHANDAN AKI CHITTAOUR
   CHAO APANAI HAATA JALAAJA JOGI

3. JALA BHALA BAYIE BHASMAKE DHEREE
   APANAY ANGALAGAJA JOGI

4. MIRAKE KE PRABHO GIRIDHARANAGHARA
   JOTA SE JOT MELAJA

MEANING

Oh Yogi, donŌt leave, donŌt leave. I fall at your feet.
I am your servant. DonŌt leave.

1. Sublime is the path of love and devotion.
   Reveal itŌs intricacies to me before you leave.

2. Oh Yogi, listen to me. I lay the prye of sandalwood.
   Before you leave, light it with your own hand and burn my body.
   Oh Yogi, donŌt leave before you burn my body in that pyre of love.

3. After it is burned to a heap of ashes,
   apply those ashes to your body.

4. Mira says, Oh my lord Giridhar,
   let my flame merge into your flame before you leave.

MUKHRAA DEKHLE PRAANEE

MUKHRAA DEKHLE PRAANEE,
ZARAA DARPAN ME
DEKHLE KITNAA PUNYA HAI KITNAA
PAAP TERE JEEVAN ME

1. KABHI TO PAL BHAR SOCHLE PRAANEE
KYAA HAI TEREE KARM KAHAANEE
PATAA LAGAALE PARE HAI KITNE
DAAG TERE DAAMAN ME

2. KHUD KO DHOKHAA DE MAT BANDE
ACHCHHE NA HOTE KAPAT KE DHADHE
SADAA NA CHALTAA KISEE KAA NAATAK
DUNIYAA KE AANGAN ME

MEANING

Oh Soul! Look at your mouth a little in the mirror.
See how much virtues and how much vices
you have accumulated in your life.

1. Oh Soul! You should reflect for a moment or two sometimes
o know the story of your deeds.
Find out how much stains there are in your clothes (in your life).

2. Oh friend, don't deceive yourself
The trade of deception and fraud in not good.
In this world the drama of any person does not last forever.

NADIYAA NA PEEYE

1. NADIYAA NA PEEYE KABHI APNAA JAL
   VRIKSH NA KHAAYE KABHI APNE PAHL
   APNE TANKAA MANKAA DHANKAA
   DOOJO KO DE JO DAAN HAI
   WO SACH-CHAA INSAAN ARE
   IS DHARTEE KAA BHAGWAAN HAI

2. AGAR SAA JISKAA ANG JALE,
   AUR DUNIYAA KO MEETHI SHVAAS DE
   DEEPAK SAA USKAA JEEVAN HAI
   JO DOOJO KO APNAA PRAKAASH DE
   DHARAM HAI JISKAA BHAGAVAD GEETAA,
   SEWAA HI VED PURAAN HAI

3. CHAAHE KO-EE GUNGAAN KARE
   CHAAHE KARE NINDAA KO-EE
   PHOOLO SE KO-I SATKAAR KARE
   YAA KAANTE CHUBH HO JAAYE KO-EE
   MAAN AUR APMAAN HI DONO
   JISKE LIYE SAMAAN HAI

MEANING

1. The river never drink its waters.
   Trees do not consume their fruits.
   Those who place their physical energy,
   mental strength and wealth at the disposal of others
   are true human beings.
   They are gods of Mother Earth.

2. Those who burn themselves like agarbhati
   and give fragence to the world,
   His or her life becomes a candle
   that luminates others lives.
   Who abide by the teachings of the Gita,
   Vedas and other texts is indeed a truthful person.

3. Whether we censure or praise such people,
   Whether we garland them with flowers
   or place thorns in their way,
   `who is unaffected by praise and censure
   is indeed a true, sincere human being.

NANDALAAL PYAARE

NANDALAL PYAARE | YASHODAA DULAARE
NAINO KAY TAARE | KAROON TIHAAREE MANUHAAR

1 PREM PIPAASAA LEKAR AAEE SUGHAR SALONEE CHHAVI
MANA ME SAMAAEE
NAA TAPA JAANOON, NAA JAPA JAANOON,
NAA PAHICHAANOON, KEVAL AASA TIHAAR.

2 AASHAA KAA BANDHAN TOOT NA JAAYE
LAGAN MILAN KEE CHHOOT NA JAAYE
OH GIRDHAAREE | OH BANAWAAREE | KRISHNA MURAAREE
|
SUNI LEHU DEEN PUKAAR |

3 TUMA BINU PAL CHHINA KAL NA PARAT HAI
BIKAL NAINA DINA RAINA JHARAT HAI
SHYAAMA SALONAA, KARI GAYO TONAA, DAI GAYO RONAA,
BAAJEE GAEE MAI HAAR |

4 KAISAY TUM BINU HAAY RAHOON MAI
KAISAY VIRAH BALAAY SAHOON MAI?
SHYAAMA BEDARDEE, KAISEE KAR DEE, AISEE KADAR KEE
JAAVAY KRIPAALU BALIHAAR.

MEANING

Oh beloved son of nanda (Krishna), Oh affectionate one of Yashoda
Oh one who is dear to the eyes I should do all I can to appease you.

1 I have come to you thirsty for love,
My mind is immersed in your charm and splendor.
I do not know of austerity, nor of japa, nor do I recognise you, I only depend on you.

2 May my faith and trust in you never be broken,
May I never loose the desire to meet you.
Oh Girdhaaree, Oh Krishna Muraaree, listen to the call of this miserable one.

3 Without you it is difficult to spend my moments
My poor eyes shed tears day and night.
Oh dear Shyaama, you have casted a spell on me and made me cry
and I lost the good fortune to be in your company.

4 How can I live without you? How can I tolerate your separation?
Oh merciless Shyaam How could you do this to one deserving appreciation
mercy and felicitation says the poet Kripaalu.

OH MAA SHYAAMA TAYREE,

OH MAA SHYAAMA TAYREE,
JO CHARANA SHARANA AAYAY
MAAYAA KEE KOWN KAHAY
MAAYAA PATI GHABARAAYAY

1. BANACHAARINA AACHARANA KO,
   SHRUTI NINDITA BATARAAYAY
   SAHACHAARI KARI UN SABA KO,
   NIJA BHUJA BHARI URA LAAYAY

2. TAWA PADA RAJA PAAWANA KO
   PAD MAAHOON LALACHAAYAY
   VRAJA LATAA VITAPA BANANO
   BRAMAAHOON MANA BHAAYAY.

3. TAYRAY ANUKAMPAA TAY
   SHIVA GOPEE BANI AAYAY
   SANAKANDI BRAHMA JNANEE
   TANA LATANA PATANA PAAYAY.

4. HAI CHAAHA KRIPAALU MAYREE
   TAYREE HEE KAHALAAYAY
   BHOOLAY BHATAKAY KABAHOON
   TABAA SEEVAA MILA JAAYAY.

MEANING

Oh Mother Shyaama, Those who seek shelter in you
Why shall they be confused about you and your creation.

1. The shrutis tell no to that barbaric, uncivilised behavior is despicable.
   Embrace and show the path of service, self study and devotion to those
   ignorance.

2. The dust of your pure lotus like feet captivates me
   I am fascinated to be like the all pervading Brahma as a weeper plant in
   Vraja Bhoomi.

3. Due to your mercy the cow herdessess took to the spiritual path
   Sanaka and others who realised your eternal nature
   relinquished their bodies in great joy.

4. I desire Oh merciful one that I should become yours.
   I who have gone off track when will I have the fortune of serving you

PINJRE KE PANCHHEE

PINJRE KE PANCHHEE RE!
TERAA DARD NA JAANE KOY
BAAHAR SE TU KHAAMOSH RAHE TO,
BHEETAR BHEETAR ROY

1. KEHNA SAKE TOO APNE KAHAANEE
   TEREE BHEE PANCHHEE KYAA ZINDAGAANEE RE
   VIDHI NE TEREE KATHAA LIKHEE
   AASOO ME KALAM DUBOY

2. CHUPKE CHUPKE RONE WAALE
   RAKHNAA CHHIPAA KE DIL KE CHHAALE RE
   YE PATTHAR KAA DESH HAI PAGLE
   KOI NA TERAA HOY

MEANING

Oh caged bird, none knows your pain.
Outwardly you appear silent and calm
but inwardly you cry in pain.

1. You can't narrate your story.
   What has become of your life Oh bird!
   Fate has written your story
   with a pen dipped in tears.

2. Oh silent mourner,
   you conceal the blister of pains in your heart.
   Oh crazy bird
   This land is one of stone hearted people.
   None will support you.
   You'll suffer alone.

PRABHU MORAY

PRABHU MORAY AVAGUNA CHITTA NA DHARO
SAMA DARASHEE HAI NAAMA TIHAARO,
CHAAHAY TO PAARA KARO

1. IKA NADYAA IKA NAARA KAHAAVAT
MAILO HEE NEERA BHARO
JABA MILA KARKE EKA BARAN BHAYAY
SURASARI NAAMA PAYO.

2. IKA LOHAA POOJAN MAY RAAKHATA
IKA GHARA BADHIKA PAYO
PAARASA GUNA AVAGUNA NAHI CHITAVATA
KANCHANA KARATA KHARO.

3. YAHA MAAYAA BHRAMA JAALA KAHAAVATA
SOORADAASA SAGARO.
ABA KEE BERA MOHI PAARA UTAARO
NAHI, PRANA JAATA TARO.

MEANING

Oh God. May I be free from impurities.
You see all with an equal eye,
You can help me to overcome sufferings.

1   It is said that the water of a small river and a gutter is filthy.
But when it combines together to from one with the River Ganga
it becomes the Ganga River.

2   We use an iron in our worshipping techniques and
iron is used to kill people as well.
The paaras stone has no defects and it makes gold more genuine.

3   Soordaas (The Poet) says that the entire creation
creates delusion for an ignorant person.
He says now at this time help me to cross this ocean of misery,
I don't want to delay it any longer.

PRABHU TERO NAAM

PRABHU, TERO NAAM
JO DHYAAWE PHAL PAAYE,
SUKH LAAYE TERO NAAM

1. TEREE DAYAA HO JAAYA TO DAATAA
   JEEWAN DHAN MIL JAAYE, MIL JAAYE,
   MIL JAAYE SUKH LAAYE TERO NAAM

2. TOO DAANEE, TOO ANTARYAAMEE
   TEREE KRIPAA HO JAAYE TO SWAAMEE
   HAR BIGREE BAN JAAYE,
   JEEVAN DHAN MIL JAAYE...

3. BAS JAAYE MERAA SOONAA ANG-NAA
   KHIL JAAYE MUR-JHAAYAA KANG-NAA
   JEEVAN ME RAS AAYE,
   JEEVAN DHAN MIL JAAYE...

MEANING

Oh Lord, your beautiful name
brings immense joy to those who sing it.

1. Oh merciful one,
   if you have your mercy and compassion
   we experience the great gift of life.

2. You are the giver,
   you are the indweller of all beings.
   Oh master, if we have your mercy
   then all our problems will be solved.

3. Come and live in my empty courtyard
   My dejected heart will blosson forth with joy
   My life will be filled with joy
   and I'll experience the wealth of life.

SANSAAR NE JAB THUKRAAYAA

SANSAAR NE JAB THUKRAAYAA, T
AB DWAAR TERE PRABHU AAYAA
MAI NE TUJHE KABHI NA DHYAAYAA,
TUNE SADAA SADAA APNAAYAA

1. MAI MAD MAAYAA ME PHOOLAA,
   TERE UPKAARO KO BHOOLAA
   TUNE KABHI NAHEE BISRAAYAA,
   MAI HEE JAG ME BHARMAAYAA

2. THAA MOH NEEND ME SOYAA,
   SHUBH AVSAR HAATH SE KHOYAA
   JAB LOOT RAHEE THEE MAAYAA,
   TUNE KITNEE BAAR JAGAAYAA

3. JAB ME SAB KUCHH KAA TERAA,
   MAI KAHTAA RAHAA MERAA MERAA
   AB ANT SAMAI JAB AAYAA,
   MAI MAN HI MAN PACHH-TAAYAA

MEANING

Oh God, I came to your door when the world forsook me.
I never thought or meditated on you
you always cared for me.

1. I was overwhelmed by the worldly intoxication and
   forgot your kindness.
   You never forgot me
   I was lost in the world.

2. I sleep in the sleep of infatuation and
   lost the golden opportunity.
   When I was obsessed by worldly possessions
   you awoke me many times.

3. Everything in this world is yours
   but I said everything is mine.
   Now the time of death is fast approaching and
   I am repenting.

AAJ ANDHERE

AAJ ANDHERRE ME HAI HAM INSAAN
GYAAN KA SOORAJ CHAMKAA DE BHAGVAAN

1. BHATAK RAHE HAME RAAH DIKHAADE
   BHAGVAN RAAH DIKHAADE
   KADAM KADAM PAR KIRAN BICHHAADE
   BHAGAVAN KIRAN BICHHAADE
   IN AKHIYAN KO PRABHU KARAADE
   JYOTI SE PEHCHAAN

2. HAM TO HAI SANTAAN TIHAARI
   PRABHU SANTAAN TIHAARI
   TEREE DAYAA KE HAM ADHIKAARI
   PRABHU HAI HAM ADHIKAARI
   DUNIYAA HOWE SUKHI HAMAAREE
   AISAA DE VARDAAN

MEANING

Today, we human beings are living
in the blinding darkness of ingnorance.
O Lord, let the lamp of your knowledge shine,
so that we can select the true path of life.

1. We are roaming in darkness;
   show us the path by shedding
   your reassuring light where we walk and
   blessing our eyes with the ability to see and select.

2. We are your own children,
   the direct inheritors of yout grand legacy of mercy.
   We are the ones privileged to enjoy
   the bounties of your grace.
   Bless us that we may enjoy
   the peace of a happy world.

NOTES

NOTES

NOTES

NOTES

NOTES

NOTES

NOTES

NOTES

NOTES